Secret Societies

FREEMASONS, ILLUMINATI AND MISSIONARIES

Taken from the Works of the Scholars of Islām

Compiled by Rasheed Barbee

ISBN: 978-1-7923-5516-5

First Edition: Jumādā ath-Thānī 1442 A.H. / February 2021 C.E.

Cover Design: Usul Design
E-mail: info@usuldesign.com

Translator: Rasheed Barbee

Editing & Formatting: Razan Gregory
annurediting.com

Publisher's Information:

Authentic Statements Publishing
P. O. Box 15536
Philadelphia, PA 19131
215.382.3382
215.382.3782-Fax

Store:
5000 Locust Street (Side Entrance)
Philadelphia, PA 19139

Website: www.authenticstatements.com
E-mail: info@authenticstatements.com

Please visit our website for upcoming publications, audio/DVD online catalog, and info on events and seminars, insha Allāh.

Transliteration Table

Consonants

ء	'	د	d	ض	ḍ	ك	k
ب	b	ذ	dh	ط	ṭ	ل	l
ت	t	ر	r	ظ	ẓ	م	m
ث	th	ز	z	ع	'	ن	n
ج	j	س	s	غ	gh	ه	h
ح	ḥ	ش	sh	ف	f	و	w
خ	kh	ص	ṣ	ق	q	ي	y

Vowels

Short		◌َ	a	◌ِ	i	◌ُ	u
Long		ـَا	ā	ـِي	ī	ـُو	ū
Diphthongs		ـَي	ay	ـَو	aw		

Glyphs

ﷺ *Sallallāhu 'alayhi wa sallam* (May Allāh's praise & salutations be upon him)

﷑ *'Alayhis-salām* (peace be upon him)

ﷻ *'Aza wa jal* (Mighty and Majestic)

ﵛ *RadiyAllāhu 'anhu* (May Allāh be pleased with him)

ﵞ *RadiyAllāhu 'anha* (May Allāh be pleased with her)

ﵟ *RadiyAllāhu 'anhum* (May Allāh be pleased with them)

ﵒ *Rahimahullah* (May Allāh have mercy upon him)

TABLE OF CONTENTS

TRANSLATOR'S FOREWORD

بِسْمِ اللَّهِ الرَّحْمَنِ الرَّحِيمِ

Secret Societies: Freemasons, Illuminati, and Missionaries is a collection of writings from the scholars of Islām, uncovering various secret societies operating within the framework to establish a new world order. The New World Order is a blueprint to unite all humanity under one government, one currency, one tribunal, and one religion; masked beneath slogans such as tolerance, diversity, and unity. Those covertly pulling the strings are the Zionist Jews. Their objective is to rebuild the Temple of Solomon, setting the stage for the appearance of their awaited Messiah, the Dajjal (anti-Christ).

Sitting on the opposite side of the chessboard are Christian missionaries. As they attempt to colonize and Christianize the globe, they work in tandem with the Zionists to establish the Jewish State of Israel. This is because they believe that three signs must precede the return of Jesus; the establishment of the State of Israel in Palestine, the occupation of Jerusalem, and the rebuilding of the Temple of Solomon on the ruins of the Al-Aqsa Mosque. For this reason, Christian evangelicals stress support for the Jewish State of Israel despite the vast ideological differences and mutual disdain between Jews and Christians.

The Muslim *'ummah* sits in the middle as a common enemy to both factions. Regrettably, as a result of heedlessness, we find some Muslims not only falling into the trap of the New World Order, but they also assist in advocating the very ploy crafted to bring about their ruin in this life and the Hereafter.

The poet said, "I acquaint myself with evil, not for the sake of evil, but to be safeguarded from it. Indeed, the person who cannot distinguish good from evil will fall into evil."

And to Allāh belongs the dominion of the heavens and the earth, and Allāh has power over all things. (Sūrah 'Āli 'Imrān 3:189)

They plot, and Allāh plans. And Allāh is the best of planners. (Sūrah al-'Anfāl 8:30)

I ask Allāh (☝) to expose the plots of the mischief-makers and grant us safety and security in this life and the Hereafter. I ask Allāh to exalt the rank of His final Prophet and Messenger (☝), and all praises belong to Allāh, the Lord of all that exists.

Rasheed Barbee

Durham, North Carolina

October 2020

THE FREEMASONS
AND ILLUMINATI

INTRODUCTION TO FREEMASONRY

Shaykh 'Alī al-Waṣīfī said:[1]

Verily, all the praises belong to Allāh. We praise Him, and we seek His assistance and His forgiveness. We seek refuge in Allāh from the evil of our souls and from the evil of our actions. Whoever Allāh guides, none can misguide him; and whoever is misguided, there is no guide for him. I bear witness that nothing has the right to be worshipped except for Allāh, alone, without partners; and I bear witness that Muḥammad is His slave and His Messenger.

As to what follows, verily, the most truthful speech is the Book of Allāh; and the best guidance is the guidance of Muḥammad (ﷺ), and the most evil of affairs are newly invented matters, and every newly invented

---

[1] Translator's note: Taken from *The Evil Reality of the Freemasons*. Shaykh 'Alī al-Waṣīfī is from the scholars of Egypt, recommended by the noble scholar Shaykh Ḥasan ibn 'Abdil Wahāb al-Banaa.

matter is an innovation, and every innovation is astray, and straying is in the Fire.

Indeed, Allāh (﷾) sent the Messenger of Allāh (ﷺ) after there was an interval between the messengers.

$$ ﴿ يَا أَهْلَ الْكِتَابِ قَدْ جَاءَكُمْ رَسُولُنَا يُبَيِّنُ لَكُمْ عَلَى فَتْرَةٍ $$

$$ مِّنَ الرُّسُلِ ﴾ ﴿١٩﴾ $$

O people of the Scripture (Jews and Christians), now has come to you Our Messenger [Muḥammad (ﷺ)] making things clear to you, after a break in (the series of) Messengers.[1]

He (ﷺ) was sent amidst people who were at odds with one another, those who worshipped idols. He was also sent to the people of the Book from the Jews and Christians. They all had different religions, and they worshipped other than Allāh (﷾). These people also had no one to guide them in their worldly affairs. They had nothing to return to in order to unite their groups and sects. So, the Prophet (ﷺ) came and invited them to the Oneness of Allāh (﷾). He was their leader; they united around him, and he (ﷺ) formed a brotherhood amongst them. Love, compassion, and brotherhood for the sake of Allāh (﷾) spread amongst them. They became allies, such that a man would form a stronger alliance with his brother in faith than the alliance he had with his blood brother. This

---

[1] Sūrah al-Mā'idah 5:19.

is because the Islāmic ideology is the greatest thing that unites the hearts and souls because it unites based upon the Oneness of Allāh (ﷻ).

Since the Prophet (ﷺ) was sent, all the nations have gathered against the religion of Islām, and they have gathered against the Muslims. From the people of the Book, there appeared various groups upon polytheism, idolatry, and deviance, while portraying themselves with a beautiful image in front of the Muslims. Some of the Muslims were deceived by this; thus, they followed them and abandoned what the Prophet (ﷺ) came with. The Prophet (ﷺ) warned against this before it happened. He (ﷺ) said,

فَإِنَّهُ مَنْ يَعِشْ مِنْكُمْ فَسَيَرَى اخْتِلَافًا كَثِيرًا، فَعَلَيْكُمْ بِسُنَّتِي وَسُنَّةِ الْخُلَفَاءِ الرَّاشِدِينَ الْمَهْدِيِينَ

Verily, he among you who lives long will see great differing, so adhere to my Sunnah and to the Sunnah of the rightly-guided caliphs.[1]

And he (ﷺ) said,

لَتَتَّبِعُنَّ سَنَنَ مَنْ قَبْلَكُمْ شِبْرًا بِشِبْرٍ، وَذِرَاعًا بِذِرَاعٍ، حَتَّى لَوْ سَلَكُوا جُحْرَ ضَبٍّ لَسَلَكْتُمُوهُ " . قُلْنَا يَا رَسُولَ اللَّهِ، الْيَهُودَ وَالنَّصَارَى قَالَ " فَمَنْ

You will certainly follow the ways of those who came before you handspan by handspan, cubit by cubit, to the extent that if

---

[1] *40 Hadith Nawawi* 28.

they entered the hole of a lizard, you will enter it too. We said, "O Messenger of Allāh, (do you mean) the Jews and the Christians?" He (ﷺ) said, "Who else?"[1]

This proves that the Jews and Christians beautify falsehood with an alluring image. So, the weak Muslims give preference to this. They unite with them, upon falsehood, under the premise that these people are only doing good deeds and trying to improve the lives of those around them.

From the modern-day groups that have deceived the Muslims is the Freemasons. They presented themselves as a group that calls to good manners and etiquette. They presented themselves as a group that calls for spreading good, serving the community, and elevating society on a socioeconomic level. While in reality, they conceal within themselves every type of evil and wickedness. They oppose each and every religion. Neither the divine revelation nor the messengers have any significance among the Freemasons. They do not give preference to one legislation above another. They do not give preference to any religion above another. They do not believe in any particular religion. Rather, they only believe, in general, that there is a creator and a god. But what are the attributes of this god? What acts of worship are due to Him? Who are the messengers and who are the followers of the messengers? What is the ideology taught by these messengers? What is the religion brought by these messengers? What is the legislation they judged by? What is

---

[1] *Bukhārī* 1397; *Muslim* 4822.

the path we should adhere to? All the above is unnecessary to the Freemasons.

It is not necessary to have a specific religion according to them. Thus, you will not find those who are Freemasons uniting under one religion. Rather, each of them remains upon his own religion. It is only necessary that they all agree that there is one God who rules the Universe. It does not matter if he is a Jew, Christian, Muslim, fire-worshipper, Hindu, or Buddhist. It only matters that he believes that there is a Lord, or there is a Creator. The Christians believe in the father and the son, and each religion has a different belief concerning their creator, but this is not important to the Freemasons. It is only important that they believe there is a Lord. As the philosophers say, "There is a deity that controls the Universe, but as for the attributes of this deity and what He wants from us, none of this is important."

The Freemasons claim to be an organization of universal brotherhood. The definition of universal brotherhood is extremely vast, such that it includes all religions and sects without giving preference to one religion or sect over another. Importance is only given to ascribing oneself to Freemasonry and remaining under the command of the Freemasons. This is what you must agree to and unite upon. You must follow the teachings and rules of the Freemasons, while your religion is a personal preference that is up to you alone. This movement unites the Jews, Christians, Muslims, Buddhists, Hindus, and others under one banner.

WHO ARE THE FREEMASONS?

Shaykh 'Abdullāh Ibn Humaid (1908-1981), the Chief Justice of Saudi Arabia and Imām of the Great Mosque of Mecca said:

All praises belong to Allāh, may Allāh elevate the rank and send peace upon the Messenger of Allāh, his family, his companions, and those who follow his guidance. As to what follows:

The Fiqh Council, in its session held in Mecca on the tenth of Shaban 1398 Hijri, corresponding to July 15, 1978, examined the issue of Freemasonry and its affiliates, as well as the Islāmic ruling concerning them.

The members of the Council conducted a comprehensive study of this dangerous organization. They read what was written about it, what was published from the Freemasons' own documents, as well as what was written and published in books, articles, and magazines by its members and some of its leaders. Based on everything that was read, the following is the undeniable conclusion.

Freemasonry is a secret organization that conceals its organization at times and openly declares it at other times, according to the circumstances of time and place. But the core principle on which it is based is secrecy in every situation. They even conceal their secrets from their members, except for exclusive members who reach a high rank within the organization.

They build relationships between their members in every part of the world based on perceived principles while concealing their true objectives from the heedless. They claim the Freemasons form a brotherhood for all their members regardless of their religious denominations, affiliations, or beliefs.

They attract those interested in joining their organization with the promise of personal benefits, on the basis that every Masonic brother will help and support all his brothers—in any part of the world—in achieving their personal goals and aspirations. If he has ambitions to become a politician, his Masonic brothers will assist him. If he gets into trouble, his Masonic brothers will assist him whether he is in the right or the wrong, whether he is oppressed or he is the oppressor. Although, they will make it appear as though he is in the right. This is from the greatest temptations that attract people to join them from various social organizations around the world. This, also, allows the Freemasons to collected significant financial contributions from them. The entry of a new member is celebrated beneath their terrorist symbol as a warning to the new member against violating instructions and the orders issued to him by hierarchy.

The heedless members are left alone to practice their religious rituals. The Masons benefit by assigning them duties from within the limits for which they are fit while keeping them in lower ranks. As for the atheists or those ready for atheism, they rise in rank based upon their experiences and repeated examinations, and their willingness to implement dangerous plans and principles.

The Freemasons have political goals, and they have a hand in most political and military coups, either openly or hidden. Their main secret objective is to oppose all religions and to destroy them collectively. They especially desire to destroy Islām within the hearts of its children.

They are keen to select affiliates with financial, political, social, or scientific status, or any position where the person can exploit their influence over society. They have no interest in affiliating with those who have no status to exploit. For this reason, they are diligent in their efforts to recruit presidents, ministers, and senior officials.

If they find a community that has an aversion to the Masonic name, they will set up locations that camouflage their name to divert attention away from themselves. The most prominent examples of this are the Lions Clubs International and the Rotary International Club. These are two Masonic organizations that have malicious principles that completely contradict and oppose the guidelines of Islām.

It has clearly been shown to all, the connection between the Freemasons and the Zionist Jews. Based on this relationship, they were able to control many Arab officials regarding the issue of Palestine. Thus, many of them shifted their efforts from the Islāmic cause to their new cause, which is the interest of the Jews and global Zionism.

Based upon this and other detailed information concerning the plots of the Freemasons, the Fiqh Council has determined this group to be from the most dangerous and destructive organizations against Islām. If a Muslim is aware of the true objectives and plots of the Freemasons, and yet he chooses to join them, then he is a disbeliever. And with Allāh (ﷻ) lies all success.[1]

---

[1] Islamic verdict 1/150-152.

ORIGIN OF THE FREEMASONS

Shaykh 'Abū Sulaymān Fuād az-Zintānī[1] said:

The Freemasons are a secret Jewish terrorist organization. They have members in every country. Some are open members, while others are secret members. The reason for its formation was to grant the Jewish community power around the globe. They called to apostasy and indecency while hiding behind false slogans such as freedom, brotherhood, and humanity. Many have been deceived by these false slogans, including some Muslims. As a result, Muslims have held conferences calling for unity of religions and universal humanity. The Freemasons is an ancient organization. Some say it was founded in the year 44 C.E. We are now in the year 2020 C.E.; thus, it was founded more than 1,970 ago. It was founded by a Roman king named Herod Agrippa. The original name of the organization was the Mysterious Force. Their initial aim was to fight against Christianity and prevent Christians from practicing their religion, as the Jews believe Judaism is the only true religion. The Jews do not believe in Jesus. How can they believe in him while they are the ones who claimed to have crucified him! Before Islām, they used to wage war against the Christians. Thus, initially, they were called the Mysterious Force. Then, centuries later, they changed their name to the Freemasons. It is comprised of the words which mean "free" and "builder," as they claim they built the temple of Solomon.[2]

---

[1] He is from the students of Shaykh Muqbil, and currently an Imām and lecturer in Ras al-Khaimah in the United Arab Emirates.

[2] "Understanding the Freemasons" lecture.

OBJECTIVES OF THE FREEMASONS

The Permanent Committee for Research and Verdicts[1] said:

The Freemasons are a secret political organization. Their goal is to eliminate religion and morality and replace them with man-made laws and a non-religious system.

They exert their efforts in provoking constant revolt and overthrowing the leadership and replacing them with another. All of this is done under the pretext of freedom of thought and belief. This is what they have clearly stated.

During the student conference of the Freemasons which convened in the year 1865, in the city of Liège (Belgium)—considered to be one of the centers of Freemasonry—it was said by one of the students, "It is a requirement that man must prevail over God and declare war on Him, and man should demolish the heavens and tear them like paper."

This is confirmed by what was mentioned in their collection of annual meetings titled *Masonic Grand Lodge 1922 Edition*. On page 98, they said, "We will strengthen the freedom of individual thought with all the powers at our disposal, and we will declare a major war against the real enemy of man, which is religion." The leaders of the Freemasons say, "Indeed the Freemasons take the human soul as its object of worship."

---

[1] Translator's note: Members at the time of this verdict include Shaykh 'Abdul Aziz ibn Baz, Shaykh 'Abdullāh al-Ghudayyan, Shaykh Ṣāliḥ Fawzān, Shaykh Bakr 'Abī Zayd, and other noble scholars.

The Freemasons are one of the most ancient secret societies that still exist. Yet, its origins are still unknown, and its goals are still unknown to many of the people. In fact, this is still unknown to many of its members. This is because their leaders are very keen to conceal their plots and deceptions. Also, due to their determination to remain secret, they did not document their goals, intentions, or purpose. Due to their secrecy, most of their affairs are conducted verbally, with no written record. When they want to write an idea or announce it to the public, it is first subjected to the scrutiny of the Masonic Censorship Committee, which decides whether or not it can be released.

The goal of the Freemasons is to destroy religion. They say, "It is not enough for us to prevail over the religious people and their places of worship; rather, our basic goal is to wipe them out of existence."

In the minutes of the World Masonic Conference in the year 1903 C.E., page 102, they issued a statement saying, "Freemasonry will take the place of religion and its lodges will take the place of places of worship." Many other statements clearly point to the intensity of their enmity toward an uncompromising war on religion.[1]

Shaykh ʿAlī al-Waṣīfī said:

The Freemasons claim their organization was established on behalf of the Jews that were expelled from Egypt during the reign of Pharaoh. Their intent is to prepare the stage for the appearance of their Christ, who is, in reality, the Anti-Christ (*Dajjal*).

---

[1] *Fatāwa al-Lajnah al-Dāʾimah* 2/312-315.

IDEOLOGY AND TACTICS OF THE FREEMASONS

Shaykh 'Abdur Razzāq Afīfī (1905-1994) said:

They disbelieve in Allāh, His Messengers, His Books, and all matters of the unseen. They consider these matters as fairytales and superstitions.

They work to topple legitimate governments and abolish the national systems of government in various countries while imposing control over them.

They legalize prostitution and use women as a means to control and manipulate men.

They work to divide non-Jews into divergent nations that remain in perpetual conflict and struggle.

They spread the poison of conflict inside a country while reviving the spirit of racism against minorities.

They destroy moral, intellectual, and religious principles while spreading chaos, terrorism, and atheism.

They use money and sex to bribe individuals and force them to join the Freemasons, especially those with high positions of authority. Their motto is "The ends justify the means."

Those who fall into their trap are surrounded from every angle, so they can be controlled. They must then execute the orders of the Freemasons as they see fit.

Those who join them must disassociate themselves from every religious, ethical, and national bond, such that their loyalty is purely for the Freemasons.

Once they have benefited from an individual and no longer need him, they can dispose of him by any means necessary.

They work to control heads of state to ensure their evil plans are implemented.

They control famous and prominent celebrities in various arts and sciences to ensure their thoughts are integrated into society.

They control the media, newspapers, and the tools of propaganda; and use them as lethal weapons. They broadcast fake news until these reports are accepted as facts in the minds of the people.

They encourage young men and women to indulge in immorality and provide them with the means to do so. They even encourage incest, weakening marital relationships, and breaking the bond of family.

They control international organizations such as the United Nations by placing Freemasons to preside over them.

They divide Muslim countries into warring factions as in the case of Sudan, which was divided into two separate factions. One method of division is to provide a tribe with weapons and coerce them into war with an opposing tribe so they can spill the blood of the children.[1]

---

[1] Aḥmad ibn ʿAlī, *The Methodology of Shaykh ʿAbdul Razzāq Afīfī and His Efforts in Establishing the Creed and Refuting Those Who Oppose It*, master's thesis.

INITIATION INTO THE FREEMASONS

Shaykh 'Alī al-Waṣīfī said:

Undoubtedly, an organization that unites people under one banner must have specific rules and guidelines for dealing with daily life, manners, and interaction with the rest of society. This group must have an ideology that each member of the Freemasons must unite upon. Consequently, there are requirements for anyone desiring to join the Freemasons. They will explain to you what the Freemasons believe, and you must agree to this belief to join the Freemasons.

The new member will have to pledge allegiance to the Freemasons. They will place a black hood over his head, covering his eyes. He will enter a dark room while blindfolded in order to give his pledge. This blindfold symbolizes the darkness the individual was upon before he embraced the Masonic way of life. Once he gives the pledge of allegiance and completes the ceremony, the blindfold is removed and the new pledge sees the light within the room. This symbolizes the light of the Freemasons which is now revealed to him. This blindfold represents how the Freemasons feel toward the ignorance of the rest of the world. They believe the entire world is blinded by darkness regardless of their religions and knowledge. Once he gives the pledge of allegiance, the blindfold is removed and he now sees the reality of everything according to their belief.

When the blindfold is removed, there are swords drawn to his neck and the Old Testament is in front of him. Now the recruit is sworn to conceal the secrets of the Freemasons. If he does not adhere to this promise willingly, he will be forced to do so. They will threaten to kill him if he exposes the secrets of the Freemasons. Most secret groups are similar to this, even those groups that ascribe to Islām.

MASONIC SYMBOLS

Shaykh 'Alī al-Waṣīfī said:

The Freemasons have secret handshakes and symbols used to identify each other when they meet, as do some Muslim organizations. Some Freemasons wear a silver ring with ten corners. They use the six-pointed star, known as the Star of David to the Jews, as their insignia. Another sign is the picture of the eye known as the Eye of Providence or the All-Seeing Eye, which sits atop the Pyramid of Khufu in Egypt. (This is the image that sits on the back of the United States one-dollar bill.)

The Freemasons' primary sign is the Square and Compass. The apparent meaning of this sign is the symbolization of an architect's tools, but there is also a secret meaning. The top of the compass, or protractor, faces the heavens while the two legs face the earth. The square under the compass also faces the earth. They claim this represents a connection between the Great Deity and the earth. They believe all their actions are in agreement with the Great Deity. For this reason, they ask the Great Deity to aid them upon their Masonic actions, beliefs, and ideologies.[1]

Masons around the world carry a small compass and a right angle because they are the symbols of Freemasonry. This is because they were

---

[1] "Understanding the Freemasons," lecture.

the main tools with which Solomon built the Holy Temple of Jerusalem, according to their claim.

Translator's Addendum

The letter G stands for the Grand Architect of the Universe. The letter G also stands for geometry, which is the basis of Freemasonry's origins.

The square and compass, when arranged together, represent six points similar to the hexagram or six-pointed star known by the Jews as the Star of David.

The twin pillars at the entrance of the Masonic lodge represent Boaz and Joachim. Freemasons believe Boaz and Joachim were two pillars made from copper and brass or bronze that stood on the porch of Solomon's Temple, the first temple in Jerusalem mentioned in the Bible.[1] Freemason General Albert Pike said, "You enter the lodge between two columns, and they represent the two which stood on the porch of the Temple, one on each side of the great eastern gateway.[2]

Tyler's sword: Outside the Masonic lodge stands a guard known as a Tyler. The sword known as Tyler's sword is depicted unsheathed across the Masonic Book of Constitutions.

The color of Freemasonry is called Masonic Blue. The color blue is to immortalize the blue flag of Israel, which bears the Star of David.

---

[1] Jeremiah 52:21-22.
[2] Albert Pike, *Morals and Dogma*, (1871).

A three-headed copper snake symbolizes the demolition of the religious, civil, and military authority of the gentiles.

———

End of Translator's Addendum

THE CONSTITUTIONS OF THE FREEMASONS

Shaykh 'Alī al-Waṣīfī said:

The Freemasons have their own constitution. The first person to author this constitution was James Anderson. This constitution was later published by the President of America, Benjamin Franklin.

Translator's Addendum

———

Dr. James Anderson (1680-1739) was a Scottish writer and ordained minister born and educated in Aberdeen, Scotland. In September of 1721, he was commissioned by the Grand Lodge to write a history of the Freemasons. It was published in 1723 as *The Constitutions of the Free-Masons*. Anderson's name does not appear on the title page, but his authorship is declared in an appendix.[1]

———

End of Translator's Addendum

---

[1] *Encyclopedia Masonica.*

THE REQUIREMENTS TO JOIN A FREEMASON LODGE

Shaykh 'Alī al-Waṣīfī said:

The stated conditions to join the Freemasons are that you must be a man.[1] You must be of sound mind, having reached the age of adulthood. Depending on the Grand Lodge, this can be anywhere from 18 to 25 years of age. You must accept the beliefs of the Freemasons. You must believe in doing acts of good and you must believe in serving society.

DEGREES OF THE FREEMASONS

"Freemasons have various degrees, meaning levels. Some deviant Islāmic groups also have degrees and levels. This is because they borrowed this methodology from the Freemasons and implemented it in Islām. The beginning degree is called the Apprentice. The next level is the Fellowcraft Mason or Second Degree. Next, there is the Master Mason or Third Degree. Once he reaches the third degree, he is entitled to all rights and privileges and can interact with Freemasons around the world. There are higher degrees, such as the 33rd degree, which is reserved for certain individuals within special sects of the Freemasons.

---

[1] Translator's note: One of the Freemasons divisions for women is The Order of the Eastern Star, a Masonic appendant body open to both men and women, established in 1850 by lawyer and educator Rob Morris. Also for women, is the Order of Job's Daughters, founded by Ethel T. Wead Mick in Omaha, Nebraska on October 20, 1920. The International Order of the Rainbow for Girls was founded for women by Reverend W. Mark Sexson in 1922.

RELATIONSHIP BETWEEN THE FREEMASONS AND THE JEWS

The Permanent Committee for Research and Verdicts said:

The principles of Freemasonry were based on theories taken from several sources, mostly from Jewish traditions. This is supported by the fact that Jewish ideas and teachings, along with their principles and symbols, were taken as the basis for the founding of the Grand Lodge in 1717 C.E.

The Freemasons still venerate the Jew Hiram[1] and they venerate the temple that he built. They also venerate the place of worship he constructed to the extent that they took it as the design of the Masonic lodges in the world.

The grandmasters of the Freemasons are Jews. They form the backbone of the Masonic movement and are the ones who represent Jewish organizations in Masonic lodges. They are responsible for the spread of Freemasonry and global cooperation between Freemasons, and they are the driving force behind Freemasonry. The Jewish elite are responsible for leading secret cells, managing their affairs, devising their plans, and secretly directing them as they wish.

This is supported by a report in the *Masonic Acacia* magazine (1908, issue number 66) which says, "There is no Masonic lodge that is free of Jews and all the Jews do not follow one way or another exclusively. Rather, there are only principles for them to follow, and this is also the case with

---

[1] Translator's note: Hiram Abiff is the central character of an allegory presented to all candidates during the third degree in Freemasonry.

the Masons. As a result, the Jewish synagogues are our [Masons'] support and we find a large number of Jews among the Freemasons."

This is also supported by what it says in the Masonic publications, that verily the Jews are certain that the best means of destroying religion is Freemasonry; and the history of the Freemasons is similar to the history of the Jews in belief.

Their symbol is the six-pointed Star of David. The Jews and the Freemasons both consider themselves to be the spiritual sons of the builders of the Temple of Solomon. The Freemasons, who distort the religion of others, open the door wide to support Judaism and its followers.

The Jews took advantage of people's simple-mindedness and good intentions, and infiltrated Freemasonry, reaching high positions within it. Thus, they breathed a Jewish spirit into the Masonic lodges and subjugated them to their own aims.

Shaykh 'Alī al-Waṣīfī said:

"Freemasons have a strong relationship with the Jews. They constantly search for centers of power around the world, and they work according to these hubs of power. They may unite with two opposing groups, so if there occurs conflict between these opposing groups and one group is defeated, the Jews will not be harmed. Sometimes you will see them in Russia and sometimes you will see them in Washington, while sometimes they will be on the side of both groups at the same time. If a war breaks out between the two opposing groups, the Jews will benefit from whichever group is victorious because they were playing both sides the entire time."

Shaykh 'Abū Sulaymān Fuād az-Zintānī said:

Rabbi Yitzhak Isaac Halevy (1847-1914) said, "Freemasonry is a Jewish institution; its history, degrees, objectives, secret symbols, and terminology are Jewish from beginning to end."[1]

Translator's Addendum

———

Rudolph Klein said in the German Masonic periodical called, *Latomia*, "Our rituals are Jewish from beginning to end, and the public must conclude from this that we have actual links with Judaism."[2]

And in his book, *Chronicles for the Children of Israel*, he said, "Indeed the emblem of the greatest British Masonic lodge is comprised of all Jewish symbols."[3]

———

End of Translator's Addendum

FREEMASONS CAUSING STRIFE AND CHAOS

The Permanent Committee for Research and Verdicts said:

One of the clearest indications of their intense desire to conceal their plans to destroy religions and provoke political revolutions is what it says in the *Protocols of the Elders of Zion*. It states, "We will concentrate these cells under a single leadership that is known to us alone. This leadership will

---

[1] "Understanding Freemasonry," lecture. Rabbi Halevy, *The Israelis of America*, (1866).
[2] *Latomia*, issue 7/7/1928.
[3] *Chronicles for the Children of Israel*, Volume 2, page 156.

be composed of our scholars, and these cells will have special representatives so that the true location of our leadership will be concealed. This leadership, alone, will have the right to decide who will speak and draw up the plans of the day. In these cells, we will plan to lay traps and snares for all the socialists and classes of revolutionary society. Most of the secret political plans are known to us and we will decide when to implement them. But the agents of the international secret police will be members of these cells. When the conspiracies start throughout the world, that will mean that one of our most dedicated agents will be at the head of these conspiracies. Of course, we will be the only people to direct the Masonic plans. We are the only people who know how to direct them and we know the ultimate goal of each action. The illiterates—meaning non-Jews—are ignorant of most of these things, especially Masonry, and they can only see the immediate results of what they are doing."

Freemasonry outwardly appears to be a call to freedom of belief, tolerance, and social reform in general. However, in reality, it is a call for permissiveness and destructive factors that cause social disintegration and the loosening of bonds between nations, destruction of religion and morals, and the spread of mischief.

Shaykh Ṣāliḥ Ṣuḥaymī said:

Protests and demonstrations are foreign to Muslims. Consequently, it is forbidden and it is falsehood. It is from the principles of the world of Zionism and the world of Freemasonry. Its origin is Judeo-Masonic.[1]

---

[1] *The Superiority of Islām.*

Shaykh ʿAlī al-Waṣīfī said:

The Freemasons have a history of causing chaos throughout the world. They started the French Revolution and financed it as well. Likewise, in modern times, the Freemasons were behind the Arab Spring uprising. Their intent is to destroy all the Muslim nations and establish weak leaders in positions of government. The Freemasons will write their constitution for them, which will be based upon American law and so-called American freedom, which has no limitations. They remove every law that is based upon the legislation of Allāh (ﷻ) because their new constitution is above all in their view. These new governments will be forced to follow the new laws. When this is in place, the countries will destroy themselves from within. These laws will grant society absolute freedom with no boundaries and no religious structure. Even a man in his own home will not have any family structure. Not only are they establishing this in the Muslim lands; but they are also establishing this within Muslim communities living among them in the West.

The first phase of the Freemasons' constitution encourages chaos among the minorities of every country. Then, they make the minorities rebel against the countries where they have resided for hundreds of years. Thus, the country will not be one united land; rather, it will be broken into pieces.

The Freemasons desire to cause division within the Muslim lands. They introduced the belief among the Muslims that they should never get angry concerning matters about Allāh (ﷻ) or the Messenger (ﷺ). They introduced the belief that Muslims should not declare allegiance to Allāh (ﷻ), His Messenger (ﷺ), or the leaders of Islām. Rather, you should become angry for the sake of your sect or party. You should become angry for the sake of your Shaykh or your scholar. The Free-masons say we need strong solutions to unite the people, but they never produce these solutions. They seek to corrupt the principles and morals of the Muslims. They raise new banners for the Muslims. They raise the banners of freedom and equality, but their banners are, in reality, nothing but lies.

Allāh (ﷻ) said about the disbelievers,

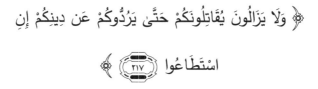

And they will never cease fighting you until they turn you back from your religion if they are able.[1]

Thus, their fighting the Muslims has no limits. They desire to push the people into polytheism, disbelief, and apostasy. Undoubtedly, to harm the religion of this *ummah* is greater than harming anything else.

The relationship between Muslim brothers is that relationship encouraged by the religion of Islām. Our religion shows us the pure way to have a disagreement. If Muslims disagree with one another in matters where deductive reasoning is allowed, no one transgresses or boycotts his brother. As for issues of ideology, then there is no disagreement in these matters.

---

[1] Sūrah al-Baqarah 2:217.

الْمُسْلِمُ أَخُو الْمُسْلِمِ

The Muslim is the brother to the Muslim.[1]

الْمُؤْمِنُونَ كَرَجُلٍ وَاحِدٍ إِنِ اشْتَكَى رَأْسُهُ تَدَاعَى لَهُ سَائِرُ الْجَسَدِ بِالْحُمَّى وَالسَّهَرِ

The believers are like one body. If his head aches, the whole body aches with fever and sleeplessness.[2]

Allāh (﷾) said,

﴿ إِنَّمَا الْمُؤْمِنُونَ إِخْوَةٌ ﴾

The believers are nothing other than brothers.[3]

Allāh (﷾) said,

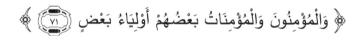

﴿ وَالْمُؤْمِنُونَ وَالْمُؤْمِنَاتُ بَعْضُهُمْ أَوْلِيَاءُ بَعْضٍ ﴾

The believing men and believing women are allies of one another.[4]

---

[1] *Tirmidhī* 1927.
[2] *Ṣaḥīḥ Muslim* 2586.
[3] Sūrah al-Ḥujurāt 49:10.
[4] Sūrah at-Tawbah 9:71.

THE MUSLIM BROTHERHOOD, EGYPT, AND THE FREE-MASONS

Shaykh 'Abdul Aziz ar-Rājihi said:[1]

Egypt is a great country, with great citizens. For this reason, Egypt has been a target throughout history for every enemy of the Islāmic nation. The Masons invaded it early on, especially after the year 1798 when it was colonized by the French. However, they left quickly in the year 1801, leaving behind Masonic monuments and their personalities. In the year 1807, England attempted to take the place of France, but they failed miserably in the face of the steadfastness of the Egyptian people. However, the Freemasons continued to eat away at the body of Egypt until they enabled the British to occupy it in 1882.

The Freemasons established massive lodges and clubs. Their members were distinguished. They had social presence and a prominent position. Classical Arabic poems were written praising them, their brotherhood, their cooperation upon goodness, their loyalty, parenting, chivalry, and secrecy. During this time, the Freemasons were not criticized at all. This was until their reality was uncovered through the great efforts of Gamāl 'Abdel Nāṣṣer, President of Egypt. In addition to their popularity, the Freemasons have a lot of experience. They are prepared for change and changing conditions. Not every Mason was known to everyone, especially those with the 33rd rank.

The weight of British occupation was extremely difficult upon the Egyptian people. After the First World War, Britain began to sense the

---

[1] *Reality of the Muslim Brotherhood.*

Egyptians were growing weary, and their anger increased until it reached its climax in 1919, the year of the famous revolution. Four years later, Britain was forced to recognize the sovereignty of Egypt and declare its constitution and parliament. However, before leaving, they planted their agents in Egypt. This was easy for Britain, seeing that it is the major Masonic country in the world and its agents have experience in this field.

Freemasonry was at its peak during this time. Its lodges and clubs were full and widespread, and its members were influential. They had newspapers and magazines that lead the cultural-intellectual movement in Egypt, such as the *Egyptian Crown Magazine*, the magazine of the elite Freemasons. In 1928, the English established an Islāmic group at the hands of a Freemason leader with the rank of 33rd degree. Men who reach this rank perform the difficult tasks; and they are intelligent, sophisticated, and cunning when it comes to politics.

This organization—new to Egypt—began playing dangerous games, ripping the society apart, striking its pillars while diverting attention away from England, until this became the people's main concern and source of anxiety. An intelligent writer, 'Abbās Maḥmoud al-Aqqād, became aware of their plot early on and wrote an article exposing their leader. While this was taking place, the State of Israel was proclaiming a state in Palestine. The British and Freemasons were shocked by the assassination of Ḥassan al-Banaa, the man they had put into position. The timing was difficult for them because the organization was not yet complete.

While the Muslim Brotherhood was fighting over the choice of a suitable successor for Ḥassan al-Banna, they were surprised by the selection of a man they did not know and had never seen before! He was never among them, nor had he ever attended a meeting with them. This man was Ḥassan al-Huḍaybī, the infamous Freemason. Everyone wondered how Ḥassan al-Huḍaybī became the leader of the Muslim Brotherhood although he was a Freemason. They wondered who placed him as the new leader.

Ḥassan al-Huḍaybī led the group for 22 years. He was able to manage the group organizationally but unable to manage it intellectually, so the group needed a more capable intellectual leadership. The group was surprised again when another man entered it whom they had never known! They also had never seen him with the first leader, Ḥassan al-Banna. He came to lead the group intellectually, although his writings before joining the group contained statements of atheism. This man was Sayyid Qutb, a 33rd degree Freemason, who would sometimes write editorials for the *Egyptian Crown Magazine*.

Under his leadership, the Muslim Brotherhood wanted to overthrow Egypt so the British could occupy it. This resulted in the 1952 coup d'état. Gamāl ʿAbdel Nāṣṣer participated in overthrowing the king of Egypt and he became president of Egypt. But he was not a Freemason and did not share the same vision as the Freemasons. Rather, he wanted to remove the British from Egypt and he wanted war with Israel, unlike the Freemasons. There was a major clash between Gamāl ʿAbdel Nāṣṣer and the group, but he forced the British to leave Egypt in 1954. He delivered his famous speech in Mansheya Square in Alexandria on the occasion of their exit. He was surprised when the Muslim Brotherhood attempted to assassinate him at the hands of Maḥmoud ʿAbdul Latīf by firing eight bullets at him, but he survived.

From this day forward Gamāl 'Abdel Nāṣṣer was at odds with the Muslim Brotherhood. He did not agree with the principle taught by Ḥassan al-Banna "We meet on what we agreed upon, and we excuse one another for what we disagreed about." The Muslim Brotherhood continued their pressure on him even during the 1967 war with Israel. 'Abdel Nāṣṣer died in 1970, while Israel occupied Sinai.

In October of 1973, the new president, Sādāt, surprised Israel with the Arab-Israeli War. King Faiṣal surprised the world at that time by cutting off oil to the West in response to the United States' aid to Israel. He stated that he did not fear an embargo from America and was prepared to return to riding donkeys and mules if aggression against Egypt did not cease. Egypt emerged victoriously and the only losers were the Jews and the Muslim Brotherhood.

On October 6, 1981, during an annual victory parade, Anwar Sādāt was assassinated in front of his army by one of his officers. The Freemasons, through their Muslim Brotherhood group, wanted to teach everyone who attempted to fight them an eloquent lesson. Whoever fought them, they will kill in the name of religion, at the hands of his own soldiers! They will make his killer a great, honorable hero and immortalize his name. And this is what happened. This group continues to play a role in the Arab lands today, such as its involvement in the Arab Spring.

IMPORTANT PERSONALITIES WITHIN THE FREEMASONS IN EUROPE

Johann Adam Weishaupt (1748-1830), founder of the Illuminati

Adam Weishaupt was the son of George Weishaupt, a Jewish rabbi in Ingolstadt, Bavaria. When his father died in 1753, he was raised under the care of his godfather who converted the family to Christianity. Adam Weishaupt enrolled in the University of Ingolstadt in Munich, Germany, where he studied law, economics, politics, history, and the occult. Thus, he was born a Jew, baptized as a Catholic, and educated by Jesuits—an order of Roman Catholic priests.

On May 1, 1776, Weishaupt founded the Order of the Illuminati, a secret society whose mission was to "oppose religious influence on society and the abuse of power by the state by fostering a safe space for critique, debate, and free speech." He adopted the name "Brother Spartacus."

Weishaupt then began to recruit members from like-minded people he had come to know at the University. One year later, Weishaupt joined a Masonic lodge and began recruiting from among the Freemasons for his secret society.[1]

Shaykh 'Abū Sulaymān Fuād az-Zintānī said:

"The second phase of the Freemasons was started around the year 1776 C.E. by the German philosopher Adam Weishaupt. He was a Christian, then he left Christianity and became a Freemason. He is the founder of the Illuminati. He founded this organization, and named it after the devil, his master."[2]

The Illuminati were named after Lucifer, which is the name used to refer to the devil.

Helena Blavatsky said:

"There is a whole philosophy of dogmatic craft in the reason why the first Archangel, who sprang from the depths of chaos, was called Lux (Lucifer), the Luminous Son of the Morning or Manvantaric Dawn. He has been transformed by the Church into Lucifer or Satan, because he is higher and older than Jehovah, and had to be sacrificed to the new dogma.[3]

---

[1] "Meet the man who started the Illuminati," *National Geographic* magazine, 07/08/2016.
[2] "Understanding the Freemasons," lecture.
[3] *The Secret Doctrine*, 129.

Adam Weishaupt quotes:

"G is Grace, the Flaming Star is the Torch of Reason. Those who possess this knowledge are indeed Illuminati."

"When man lives under government, he is fallen, his worth is gone, and his nature tarnished."

"I am proud to be known to the world as the founder of the Illuminati."

"At a time, however, when there was no end of making game of and abusing secret societies, I planned to make use of this human foible for a real and worthy goal, for the benefit of people. I wished to do what the heads of the ecclesiastical and secular authorities ought to have done by virtue of their offices."[1]

Léon Blum (1872-1950)

Shaykh 'Abū Sulaymān Fuād az-Zintānī said:

"In France, there was also Léon Blum. He was Jewish, a French socialist politician, and a three-time prime minister. He was entrusted with spreading pornography. He authored a book entitled *Marriage*, and you will not find a book more vulgar than it.

Jean-Jacques Rousseau (1712-1778)

Shaykh 'Abū Sulaymān Fuād az-Zintāni said:

---

[1] Schneider and Heinrich, *Quest for Mysteries: The Masonic Background for Literature in 18th Century* (Germany).

"Also, among their prominent figures were Jean-Jacques Rousseau, a Genevan philosopher in France. In addition to being a Freemason, he was a member of the Society of the Jacobins. Commonly known as the Jacobin Club, it became the most influential political club during the French Revolution of 1789. The period of its political ascendancy includes the Reign of Terror, during which time well over 10,000 people were put on trial and executed in France, many for political crimes."[1]

Karl Marx (1818-1883)

Shaykh 'Abū Sulaymān Fuād az-Zintānī said:

"Karl Marx, a German philosopher, and Friedrich Engels, both reached the 31st degree in the ranks of the Freemasons."[2]

François-Marie Arouet (1694-1778)

Shaykh 'Abū Sulaymān Fuād az-Zintānī said:

François-Marie Arouet was known by his pen name, Voltaire. He was a deist[3] who wrote books attacking Islām and religion in general.

---

[1] "Understanding the Freemasons," lecture.
[2] "Understanding the Freemasons," lecture.
[3] Translator's note: Deism is the philosophical position that rejects revelation as a source of religious knowledge and asserts that reason and observation of the natural world are sufficient to establish the existence of a supreme being or creator of the Universe.

Translator's Addendum

———

Cecil Rhodes (1853-1902), Rhodes Scholarship to establish the New World Order

Cecil Rhodes was the Prime Minister of the Cape Colony, now located in present-day South Africa. He made his fortune by investing in the diamond mines of Africa. He was also the architect of apartheid and a white supremacist.

Rhodes was initiated into Freemasonry at Apollo Lodge #357 in September 1877 at the age of 24. He sought to create one land—Rhodesia—from Cape Town to Cairo. It would be run by the Freemasons and inspired by the legend of King Solomon that he spoke of often in the lodge. He formed a secret society within the Freemasons that he called the Round Table and the Society of the Elect. In his last will and testament, he founded the Rhodes Scholarship. The scholarship enables male students from territories under British rule—or formerly under British rule—and from Germany, to study at Rhodes' alma mater, the University of Oxford. He financed the Rhodes Scholars at Oxford University for these chosen scholars to build an empire of worlds.[1]

Madame Helena Blavatsky (1831-1891)

Helena Blavatsky was a Russian occultist and philosopher. She studied Sufism, Coptic Christianity, and the Druze order. She traveled to Canada, the United States, Mexico, South America, the West Indies, Tibet,

---

[1] Graeme Kilshaw, *Secret Societies, Politics, Power, and Wealth.*

India, and Sri Lanka to learn from Buddhist and Hindu mystics, magicians, and spiritualists.

She was also a Freemason. Her Masonic diploma, dated the 24th of November 1877, reads:

"We, the Thrice-Illustrious Sovereign Grand Master General... do declare and proclaim our illustrious and enlightened Brother,[1] H.P. Blavatsky, to be an Apprentice, Companion, Perfect Mistress, Sublime Elect Scotch Lady, Grand Elect, Chevalière de Rose Croix, Adonaite Mistress, Perfect Venerable Mistress, and a Crowned Princess of Rite of Adoption."[2]

In 1887, she published a monthly magazine called *Lucifer* to bring to light the hidden things of darkness.

On September 7, 1875, she founded a society called The Theosophical Society. Their stated objectives were:

1. To form the nucleus of the Universal Brotherhood of Humanity, without distinction of race, religious creed, gender, caste, or color.
2. To encourage the study of Comparative Religion, Philosophy, and Science.
3. To investigate unexplained laws of Nature, and the powers latent in man.[3]

---

[1] Translator's note: They referred to the women in their society as "brother."
[2] *Universal Freemasonry Famous Freemasons.*
[3] *Theosophia* (Los Angeles, California: 1968).

Helena Blavatsky said, "Masonry has played and is still playing an important part in the world. It was through Masonry and Masons that the United States of America was made possible."[1]

Helena Blavatsky traveled in search of ancient wisdom and mysterious cults throughout Egypt. There, she would meet a mysterious man and learn about a secret book called *Chaldean Book of Numbers*. The man she met was Jamāl al-Dīn al-Afghānī. She referred to him as Serapis Bey, one of the Secret Chiefs.

End of Translator's Addendum

---

[1] *Isis Unveiled* (1877), *The Secret Doctrine* (1888), *The Voice of the Silence* (1889), *The Key to Theosophy* (1889).

IMPORTANT PERSONALITIES WITHIN THE FREEMASONS IN THE ISLĀMIC WORLD

In the Arab world, Freemasonry probably played its most significant role in terms of impact and consequences, as an instrument of Western infiltration in the fields of society, culture, and ideology.[1]

Jamāl al-Dīn al-Afghānī (1839-1897)

He was a political activist from Afghanistan and a member of the Freemasons. He joined a Masonic lodge called the Eastern Star and, in December of 1877, he was elected Grand Master of this lodge.[2] He wrote the following letter in 1875, requesting entry into the Masonic lodge. "I, the undersigned, a teacher of philosophical sciences, Jamāl al-Dīn al-Kābulī, aged 37, ask the Brethren of Purity, call on the faithful

---

[1] Barbara De Poli, *Freemasonry and the Orient: Esotericisms Between the East and the West.*

[2] *Shalash, Al-Yahūd wa-Almā Sūna,* 226-7.

companions, guides of the sacred Masonic organization, to be willing and favorable to accept me in that pure organization, and to let me enter the body of the affiliates of that glorious association."[1]

Shaykh Muqbil bin Hādī said about him:

"The principles and foundations of Bahá'í Faith are consistent with many principles and objectives of Jamāl al-Dīn. In addition to the followers of Bahá'í Faith being affected by the Sufi belief that Allāh is incarnate and part of His creation, they are also affected by the Masonic belief of uniting all religions into one. We can mention Jamāl al-Dīn's message to the French Masonic lodge, and the Masonic lodge selecting him as their president, as proof of his position within the Freemasons."[2]

Muḥammad 'Abduh (1849-1905)

He was an Egyptian writer and student of Jamāl al-Dīn al-Afghānī. At the age of 28, he joined a Masonic lodge called Planet of the East.

Shaykh Muqbil said about him:

He is an opinionated man, and we do not call him an intellectual because the sound intellect does not oppose the sound text. And it is affirmed that he joined the Freemasons. He is from the reasons the Egyptian people were diluted and weakened. He criticized the evidence of prophecy and the stories of the prophets. He, likewise, criticized many aspects

[1] Mahdavi Afshar documents.
[2] Shaykh Muqbil, *The Volcano in Blowing Up the Thought of Unity of Religion.*

of the Islāmic legislation. In his book *Tafsir Manar*, he said Jesus will not descend to earth during the last days. While the Prophet (ﷺ) said,

وَالَّذِي نَفْسِي بِيَدِهِ لَيُوشِكَنَّ أَنْ يَنْزِلَ فِيكُمُ ابْنُ مَرْيَمَ حَكَمًا مُقْسِطًا فَيَكْسِرَ الصَّلِيبَ وَيَقْتُلَ الْخِنْزِيرَ وَيَضَعَ الْجِزْيَةَ

By the One in Whose Hand is my soul, the son of Maryam shall soon descend among you, judging justly. He shall break the cross, kill the pig, remove the tax of protection.[1]

Muḥammad 'Abduh also said the Dajjal (anti-Christ) is a fairy tale symbol. I believe if this man were alive during the era of Imām Aḥmad, may Allāh have mercy upon him, Imām Aḥmad would have judged him to be a heretic."[2]

Mustafa Kemal Atatürk (1881-1938)

He was the first president of the Republic of Turkey and a Freemason. The Dean of Freemasonry in the Middle East, Hanā 'Abū Rasheed, said, "The Turkish coup d'état of 1918 C.E. by the great brother Mustafa Kemal Atatürk, was the most important thing by the immortal Turkish hero."

---

[1] *Jami' at-Tirmidhī* 2233.
[2] Shaykh Muqbil, fatāwa.

Shaykh 'Abū 'Amār 'Alī al-Huḍayfī said about him:

Secularism moved from theory to practice in the Arab world with the fall of the Ottoman Islāmic Caliphate in 1924 C.E. at the hands of the disguised Jew Mustafa Kemal Atatürk. Mustafa Kemal Atatürk was a Dönmeh Jew. (The Dönmeh were a group of Sabbatean[1] crypto-Jews in the Ottoman Empire who converted publicly to Islām but retained their beliefs in secret.)

He pretended to be Muslim while hiding his hypocrisy. He would pray in the front row of the army and flatter the scholars. When the opportunity presented itself, he went against the Ottomans. Then he carried out a great revolution that ended with the separation of Turkey from the rest of the Ottoman Empire.

Mustafa Kemal Atatürk abolished the Islāmic Caliphate and openly declared it an atheist secularist state. He closed many mosques, prohibited the call to prayer in the Arabic language, and persecuted the scholars in the most horrific way. Dozens were killed and hung from trees. He forced the people to abandon Islāmic attire, forced them to wear European clothes, and canceled all religious endowments. He prevented prayer in the Hagia Sophia Grand Mosque and turned it into a museum.

In addition, he abolished Sharī'ah law and imposed Switzerland civil laws. He eliminated Islāmic education and banned Qur'ān schools. He replaced the Arabic language with Latin script. He prohibited polygamy

---

[1] Translator's note: The Sabbateans were a variety of followers of disciples and believers in Sabbatai Zevi (1626-1676), a Jewish rabbi who was proclaimed to be the Jewish Messiah in 1666.

and divorce. He made the inheritance equal between men and women. He abolished the use of the Hijri calendar, and placed the Gregorian date in its place. He encouraged young men and women to engage in prostitution and immorality. He made several evil practices lawful. Rather, he was an example of immorality, corruption, and alcoholism. When the foreign occupation left the Arab and Islāmic countries, he was keen not to hand over the reins of power to anyone except those who had rejected Islām and did not want the country to implement Islām. Thus, these groups waged war against Islām from every direction.[1]

Sayyid Qutb (1906-1966)

Sayyid Qutb studied Freemasonry and took much of his ideology from its teachings before he traveled to the United States.

Sayyid Qutb said, "I became a Freemason because I was (already) a Freemason, yet I was in need of polishing and refinement. Hence, I chose this straight path so I could leave the importance of polishing and refinement to the hand of Freemasonry. What an excellent hand and how excellent are the Freemasons."[2]

Shaykh Rabee' said about Sayyid Qutb:

Sayyad Qutb would read the works of Western philosophers. He traveled to the West and to America, where he stayed for two years. While there, he learned Freemasonry, Judaism, Christianity, Communism, and all the religions. He learned every type of evil and immorality. He stayed there

---

[1] "The Dangers of Secularism," lecture.
[2] "Why I Became a Freemason," *Al-Taj al-Masri*, 04/23/1943.

for two years, then he returned to the Islāmic east. Upon his return, he became an overseer of a revolution that shook Islām. The people elevated him as leader of the ʿummah. He insulted the prophets. He also insulted the companions and declared some of them to be disbelievers. He insulted the Islāmic ʿummah, declaring them as disbelievers.[1]

---

[1] "Adhere to the Book and the Sunnah," lecture.

IMPORTANT PERSONALITIES WITHIN THE FREEMASONS IN AMERICA

Shaykh 'Alī al-Waṣīfī said:

The largest gathering of Freemasons is in the United States of America, in the city of Oak Brook, Illinois. Here you will find two organizations, the Lions Clubs International and the Rotary International Club.[1] The Lions Club is a reference to Solomon's Temple (☰) which the Jews claim exists in modern-day Palestine. This shows the relationship between the Freemasons and the Jews. The Rotary Club is so named due to them constantly rotating their meetings to different locations, such as the homes or offices of different members. This rotation can also be found among some groups that ascribe to Islām. These groups meet within the homes of its members while avoiding the masjid, the house of Allāh (☰), and turning the people away from it.

---

[1] Translator's note: The Rotary Club International's headquarters resides in Evanston, Illinois, 26 miles from Oak Brook.

General Albert Pike (1809-1891), high ranking official in the Ku Klux Klan

Shaykh 'Abū Sulaymān Fuād az-Zintānī said:

"In America, General Albert Pike lead the revival of the Freemasons. After he was forced to resign from the military, he poured his hatred upon the people through Freemasonry."

Albert Pike was also a high-ranking official in the Ku Klux Klan. Regarding membership in the Freemasons, Pike is quoted as saying, "I took my obligation to white men, not to negroes. When I have to accept negroes as brothers or leave Masonry, I shall leave it!"[1]

Translator's Addendum

Many of America's founding fathers, to include 9 signers of the Declaration of Independence and 14 U.S. presidents, belonged to the Freemasons. George Washington, Paul Revere, Mark Twain, abolitionist John Brown, former president Harry S. Truman, former F.B.I. director J. Edgar Hoover, General of the Army Douglas MacArthur, and astronaut John Glenn were all Freemasons. Henry Ford, Founder of the Ford Motor Company, belonged to Palestine Lodge No 357, in Detroit.

End of Translator's Addendum

---

[1] Grand Lodge of the State of New York (1899).

Joseph Smith (1805-1844), founder of the Mormons Church of Latter-day Saints

Joseph Smith was an American religious leader and founder of Mormonism and the Latter-day Saint movement. Joseph Smith claimed to be a prophet, saying he had a dream in which an angel directed him to a buried book of golden plates inscribed with a Judeo-Christian history of an ancient American civilization. In 1830, Smith published what he said was an English translation of these plates called the Book of Mormon. The same year, he organized the Church of Christ, calling it a restoration of the early Christian church. Members of the church were later called Latter Day Saints or Mormons.

In 1842, Smith was raised to the third degree of Master Mason "on sight" by Grand Master Jonas of the Grand Lodge of Illinois.[1] Terry Chateau said, "The Joseph Smith family was a Masonic family that lived by and practiced the estimable and admirable tenets of Freemasonry. The father, Joseph Smith, Sr., was a documented member in Upstate New York. He was raised to the degree of Master Mason on May 7, 1818, at Ontario Lodge No. 23 of Canandaigua, New York. An older son, Hyrum Smith, was a member of Mount Moriah Lodge No. 112 in Palmyra, New York."[2]

Mormons share many similarities with Freemasonry, such as symbols, signs, vocabulary, and clothing. These similarities include robes, aprons,

---

[1] *Joseph Smith, History of the Church*, Volume 4, Chapter 32, page 552.
[2] Terry Chateau, *"Freemasonry and the Church of Latter-day Saints,"* (2001).

handshakes, and ritualistic raising of the arms.[1] They give their own interpretations to these symbols to fit the Mormon narrative.

After a major dispute within the Mormon church, Joseph Smith was arrested for inciting a riot. While incarcerated, an armed mob stormed the Carthage Jail, killing Hyrum Smith instantly. Joseph Smith was shot as he attempted to jump from a window. As he lay dying, his last words were "Is there no help for the widow's son?" This is a phrase used as an appeal for help from a Freemason in trouble to brother Masons.

Brigham Young (1847-1877), founder of Brigham Young University

Brigham Young was the successor to Joseph Smith as leader of the Mormon church. He founded Brigham Young University in Utah. He was initiated into Freemasonry in 1842.

William Miller (1782-1849), Seventh-day Adventists

William Miller was a Freemason member of the Grand Lodge of Vermont and a Baptist preacher.[2] He started a religious movement known as Millerism. He proclaimed that the second coming of Jesus would occur soon and said, "My principles, in brief, are that Jesus Christ will come again to this earth, cleanse, purify, and take possession of the same, with all the saints, sometime between March 21, 1843, and March 21, 1844."[3] March 21st passed without incident, and further discussion and study resulted in

---

[1] *Goodwin*, 54-59 (1920).

[2] *The American Lodge of Research Free and Accepted Masons.* vol. iii, no. 1, (October 31, 1938 - October 30, 1939).

[3] Everett N. Dick, *William Miller and the Advent Crisis.*

the brief adoption of a new date of April 18, 1844. Like the previous date, April 18th passed without the return of Jesus. Miller responded publicly, writing, "I confess my error, and acknowledge my disappointment; yet I still believe that the day of the Lord is near, even at the door."[1] After the failure of Miller's expectations for October 22, 1844, the date became known as the Millerites' Great Disappointment. New heirs of his message emerged, including the Advent Christians (1860), the Seventh-day Adventists (1863), and other Adventist movements.

Charles Taze Russell (1852-1916), Jehovah's Witnesses

Charles Russell was a pastor and founder of what was then known as the Bible Student movement. After his death, his followers adopted the name Jehovah's Witnesses. Russell was influenced by the writings of William Miller of the Seventh-day Adventists. Russell founded the Zion's Watch Tower Tract Society to promote his teachings. Jehovah's Witnesses believe that Jesus is God's only direct creation, that everything else was created by way of Jesus. He is described as the "exact representation of God." Jehovah's Witnesses believe only 144,000 will enter Paradise and they do not believe in Hell.

In an address delivered in a San Francisco Masonic hall in 1913, Russell said, "Now, I am a free and accepted Mason. I trust we all are. But not just after the style of our Masonic brethren." He went on to say, "True Bible believers may or may not belong to the Masonic fraternity, but they are all Masons of the highest order since they are being fashioned,

---

[1] Sylvester Bliss, *Memoirs of William Miller*.

chiseled, and polished by the Almighty to be used as living stones in the Temple Built Without Hands."[1]

William Saunders Crowdy (1847-1908), founder of the Black Hebrew Israelites

William Saunders Crowdy was born in St. Mary's County, Maryland on August 11, 1847. At age 16, he joined the United States Army and served in the Civil War from 1863 to 1865. William Crowdy moved to Kansas around 1890, after spending 25 years in Oklahoma, where he became both a Prince Hall Freemason and deacon in the Baptist Church.

On September 13, 1892, Crowdy claimed to have had several visions in which he was told that Blacks were descendants of the ten lost tribes of Israel. He proceeded to create the Church of God and Saints of Christ and is regarded as a founder of the Black Hebrew Israelite movement.

Marcus Garvey (1887-1940)

Marcus Garvey, born in Saint Ann's Bay, Jamaica, was a Pan-Africanist and founder of the Universal (United) Negro Improvement Association and African Communities League. Marcus Garvey was a member of Prince Hall Freemasonry. Prince Hall Freemasons is the world's first lodge of black freemasonry. Prince Hall (1735-1807) is considered the founder of black freemasonry in the United States, known today as Prince Hall Freemasonry.[2]

---

[1] Dr. Leslie W. Jones, "The Temple of God Souvenir Notes," (1913).
[2] "Africans in America," WGBH-TV, (Boston).

Noble Drew Ali (1886-1929), founder of the Moorish Science Temple

Born in North Carolina, Timothy Drew, better known as Noble Drew Ali, founded the Moorish Science Temple of America. When Jamāl al-Dīn al-Afghānī and Muḥammad 'Abduh traveled to America in the winter of 1882 to propagate the doctrine of Ancestral Pride and Sufism, Eliza Turner and John Drew Quitman—the parents of Drew Ali—studied under him. He entered the Drew family into the Asiatic Brethren, a German Masonic organization. As a teenager, Timothy Drew traveled to Egypt to study among the students of Jamāl al-Afghānī and Muḥammad 'Abduh. The Moorish Science Temple would later be founded upon the teachings of Sufism learned from Jamāl al-Dīn al-Afghānī.[1] Drew is said to have also studied at the old Pontifical Ethiopian College in Vatican City.

Timothy Drew was a member of Ancient Egyptian Arabic Order Mystic Shrine and the Ahmadiyya cult. He also became a high-level Shriner and member of the Grotto under Dr. Sulaiman's Medina-Mecca Temple. He incorporated many Masonic teachings into the doctrine of the Moorish Science Temple and designed their temple to resemble Masonic lodges. Drew Ali said, "Try to have your temples in buildings where the meetings are on the second floor, like the Masons."[2] In his book, *Circle Seven Koran*, he plagiarized chapters 20 through 45 from the work *Unto Thee I*

---

[1] The Moorish American prophet noble Drew Ali Professor Ravanna Bey.
[2] Noble Drew Ali, *Oral Statements and Prophecies Prophet*.

Grant, written by a Masonic order known as the Rosicrucian Order.[1] He even borrowed the title Noble from Masonic rituals.

David Ford-El (Dates unknown), founder of Nation of Islām

David Ford-El, also known as Wallace Fard Muḥammad, was the founder of the Nation of Islām. He was previously a member of the Ahmadiyya, the Freemasons, and the Moorish Science Temple. Upon the death of Drew Ali, he claimed to be the rightful successor but was denied. Consequently, he established a new cult.

Elijah Muḥammad (1897-1975), leader of Nation of Islām

An article written in the *Final Call Magazine* addresses Elijah Muḥammad's claim to the true teachings of Freemasonry, as written in his book *The Secrets of Freemasonry* and discussed in his lectures. Mother Tynnetta Muḥammad[2] said, "Elijah Muḥammad addressed this topic of Masonry in several places in his "Theology of Time" lecture series. On June 11, 1972, standing in Mosque Maryam, he spoke at length to the Black Masons in particular, with an explanation of what they are currently given in their degree program under the White Masonic Order. He stated that while reading a book on ancient masonry at the Congressional Library in Washington, D.C., he often mused over what they were teaching that withheld some of the secret inner meanings of their

---

[1] Kambiz Ghaneabassiri, *A History of Islam in America: From the New World to the New World Order*, (2010).
[2] Tynnetta Muḥammad (1941 –2015) was a secretary and wife of Elijah Muḥammad.

rituals and ceremonies, the truth of which he was well taught by his master teacher W. F. Muḥammad, the Great Mahdi.[1]

Louis Farrakhan (1933 to present), leader of the Nation of Islām

Louis Farrakhan, the current leader of the Nation of Islām, is also an honorary Freemason. An article in the *Final Call* states, "Several Black Masonic jurisdictions came together on September 28th to bestow the highest honors, accolades, and respect upon Minister Louis Farrakhan of the Nation of Islām during a special gathering at the Palace, home of Elijah Muḥammad." "These are the highest honors that can be bestowed upon a Mason," explained Tony Hawkins of John G. Jones Grand Lodge of California Ancient Free and Accepted Masons.[2]

Dwight York (1945 - present), founder of Nuwaubian Nation

Dwight York is known by several aliases, including Malachi Z. York.[3] He established the Nuwaubian Nation. The Nuwaubian Nation established their own brand of Freemasonry known as The Sabaean Grand Lodge. In this lodge, York is given the title of Sovereign Grand Commander. In traditional Freemasonry, the highest honor given is the 33rd degree; however, within the Sabaean Grand Lodge, York's degree is recognized as 33°/720°.[4]

---

[1] Mother Tynnetta Muḥammad, *Masonry and the Nation of Islām Revealed Through the Divine Teachings of the Honorable Elijah Muḥammad*.

[2] "Brotherhood of Black Masons Bestow Honors," *The Final Call*, October 2, 2019.

[3] Dwight York was convicted of over 100 counts of child molestation. He is currently imprisoned in Colorado. His projected release date is July 12, 2120.

[4] "Grand Edits," The Sabaean Grand Lodge.

FREEMASONS AND THE MUSIC INDUSTRY

Wolfgang Amadeus Mozart (1756-1791), musician and composer

Shaykh 'Abū Sulaymān Fuād az-Zintānī said:

"Freemasonry has a close relationship with the music industry, so they often express their ideas and principles in the form of music. Among the most famous members of the Freemasons and Illuminati is Wolfgang Amadeus Mozart. Mozart was initiated into the Vienna Freemasons in December 1784. Mozart, along with German composer Emanuel Schikaneder, composed his famous piece "The Magic Flute" during a time when Freemasonry was frowned upon. Mozart and Schikaneder filled "The Magic Flute" with Masonic symbolism. Mozart also composed the piece "Masonic Funeral Music."[1]

---

[1] "Understanding the Freemasons," lecture.

FREEMASONRY AND SATANISM

General Albert Pike, a leader among the Freemasons, said, "That which we must say to the crowd is, 'We worship a god, but it is the god one adores without superstition. To you, Sovereign Grand Inspector General, we say this—and you may repeat it to the brethren of the 32nd, 31th, and 30th degrees—the Masonic religion should be by all of us initiates of the high degrees, maintained in the purity of the luciferin doctrine.'"[1]

Helena Blavatsky said, "Once the key to Genesis is in our hands, the scientific and symbolical Kabalah unveils the secret. The Great Serpent of the Garden of Eden and the Lord God are identical, and so are Jehovah and Cain."[2]

RULING ON MUSLIMS JOINING THE MASONS

---

[1] A.C. De La Rive, *La Femme et L'enfant dans La Franc-Maconnerie Universelle*, 588.
[2] *The Secret Doctrine*, 582.

The Permanent Committee for Research and Verdicts said:

Based on the reality of the Freemasons that we have mentioned, any Muslim who joins a Masonic group, knowing the true nature of Free-masonry and its secrets, and carries out its rituals and is keen to do so, is a disbeliever who should be asked to repent. If he repents, then this is good. Otherwise, the Muslim ruler has the right to execute him. If he dies in that state, then his recompense will be that of the disbelievers.

Whoever joins the Freemasons but does not know what they really are—their plots against Islām and the Muslims, along with their spreading evil and the evil that they are planning against everyone who tries to bring people together and reform nations—and he joins them in their general activities and talk that does not apparently contradict Islām, then this person is not a disbeliever. Rather, he is excused, in general, because of them concealing their true nature from him and him not sharing their basic beliefs in creed. He, also, does not share their goals, nor did he map out the way for them to achieve their vile goals.

The Prophet (ﷺ) said, "Verily actions are only based upon the intentions, and each person will have that which they intended.

But it is a must that he disavows himself from the Freemasons when he finds out what they are about. He must expose their reality to the people and strive to spread their secrets and plots against the Muslims so that this will be a disgrace for them and undermine their efforts.

Therefore, it is necessary that the Muslim surround himself with good people who will cooperate with him in his religious and worldly affairs. He should be far-sighted in choosing close friends so that he will be safe from being tempted by their seemingly attractive ideas and the evil consequences of their sly words. As a result, he will not fall into the traps of the people of shirk who set these traps to ensnare those who are easily deceived, follow their whims and desires, and are weak in reasoning. With Allāh (﷾) lies all success and may the peace and blessings of Allāh (﷾) be upon our Prophet Muḥammad (ﷺ), his family, and his companions.[1]

SKULL AND BONES SOCIETY

The Skull and Bones Society is one of the reputed "Big Three" societies at Yale, along with the Scroll and Key Society and Wolf's Head Society. It was founded in 1832 by William H. Russell, a student at Yale University. He came from a wealthy family. His family owned Russell & Company, and they control the opium trade empire in America. This organization is also known by other names such as Order 322 and The Brotherhood of Death. Their insignia consists of two leg bones beneath a skull; at the bottom is the number 322. The number 322 refers to the year Greek Statesman Demosthenes died. His death was a turning point in the transformation of ancient Athens from democracy to plutocracy. (Plutocracy is a society that is ruled or controlled by the wealthy.) Several politicians and prominent figures were Bonesmen, such as William Howard Taft, the 27th President of the United States; Prescott Bush, former United States Senator; his son George H. W. Bush, 41st President of the United States; his grandson George W. Bush, 43rd President

---

[1] *Fatāwa al-Lajnah al-Dā'imah* 2/312-315.

of the United States; as well as John Kerry, former United States Senator. Skull and Bones alumni also include federal judges and supreme courts justices, Rabbis and ministers, actors and athletes, CIA agents, professors, doctors, and bankers.

THE KNIGHTS TEMPLAR

The Knights Templar were soldiers dedicated to protecting Christian pilgrims to the Holy Land during the Crusades. The military order was founded around 1118 when Hugues de Payens, a French knight, created the Poor Fellow-Soldiers of Christ and the Temple of Solomon, or The Knights Templar for short. The Knights Templar symbol is the Cross of Lorraine, a double-barred cross that is featured prominently in the coat of arms of the Dukes of Lorraine. It is named after Lorraine Nobleman Godfrey de Bouillon who became the king of Jerusalem during the First Crusade. This symbol is the emblem for the American Lung Association and Exxon Mobil Corporation.[1]

SHRINERS INTERNATIONAL

Shriners International, also commonly known as The Shriners—formerly known as the Ancient Arabic Order of the Nobles of the Mystic Shrine—is a Masonic society that was established in 1870. The Shriners was started by two Freemasons, Walter M. Fleming and William J.

---

[1] Jessica Pearce Rotondi, *Five Secret Societies That Have Remained Shrouded in Mystery.*

Florence, who wanted to start a group of Masons centered on fun and fellowship more than ritual. William Florence took the Arab theme of the Shriners after being invited to a party by an Arab diplomat. The first temple established was Mecca Temple, established at the New York City Masonic Hall on September 26, 1872.

THE SHRINERS' RECOGNITION TEST

Shriners recognize each other with a lengthy series of questions and answers, such as:[1]

Question: Have you traveled any?

Answer: I have.

Question: From where to what place have you traveled?

Answer: Traveled east over the hot burning sands of the desert.

Question: Where were you stopped at?

Answer: At the devil's pass.

Question: What were you requested to do?

Answer: I was requested to contribute a few drops of urine.

Question: Why were you requested to do this?

---

[1] Erza A. Cook, *Ancient Arabic Order of the Nobles of the Mystic Shrine.*

Answer: As a token of my renouncing the wiles and evils of the world and being granted permission to worship at the Shrine.

Question: At what shrine did you worship?

Answer: At the Shrine of Islām.

ORDER OF THE ROSE CROSS

Order of the Rose Cross, also known as the Rosicrucian Order, is based upon Rosicrucianism, a spiritual and cultural movement that arose in Europe in the early 17th century after the publication of three manifestos announced the existence of a previously unknown esoteric order to the world.[1] This order was founded by Christian Rosenkreuz (1378-1484), a native of Germany also known as Christian Rose Cross. The manifestos were titled "The Fame of the Brotherhood of RC," "The Confession of the Brotherhood of RC," and the "Chymical Wedding of Christian Rosicross anno 1459." The manifestos speak of a German doctor and mystic philosopher referred to as Father Brother C.R.C. (Christian Rosenkreuz). He is said to have lived for 106 years, traveling to the Middle East to study with Christian mystics and Sufis. During his lifetime, the order had eight members, each a doctor sworn to celibacy.

---

[1] Frances A. Yates, *The Rosicrucian Enlightenment.*

THE GEORGIA GUIDESTONES CONNECTION TO THE ORDER OF THE ROSE CROSS

The Georgia Guidestones, often referred to as the American Stone-henge, is a monument in Elbert County, Georgia. In June 1979, an elderly man arrived in Elbert County, Georgia and introduced himself as R.C. Christian, an alias and reference to Christian Rosenkreuz, the founder of the Order of the Rose Cross. He purchased five acres of land from farm owner Wayne Mullinex and built a structure comprised of a compass, calendar, clock, and pillars.

Each pillar was engraved with a set of guides written in eight of the world's languages, English, Spanish, Swahili, Hindi, Hebrew, Arabic, Chinese, and Russian. Each pillar is sixteen feet tall and weighs over twenty tons apiece. The capstones contain script in classical Greek and Egyptian hieroglyphics. Six feet beneath the structure lies a time capsule. The text written on the pillars contains the following ten directives.

1. Maintain humanity under 500,000,000 in perpetual balance with nature.[1]
2. Guide reproduction wisely, improving fitness and diversity.
3. Unite humanity with a living new language.
4. Rule passion, faith, tradition, and all things with tempered reason.
5. Protect people and nations with fair laws and just courts.

---

[1] Translator's note: The world population in 2020 is 7.8 billion. This directive suggested maintaining humanity at half a billion.

6. Let all nations rule, internally resolving external disputes in a world court.
7. Avoid petty laws and useless officials.
8. Balance personal rights with social duties.
9. Prize truth, beauty, love, and seeking harmony with the infinite.
10. Be not a cancer on the earth. Leave room for nature. Leave room for nature.

THE NEW WORLD ORDER—ONE WORLD RELIGION

Shaykh Bakr 'Abī Zayd said:

The vilest conspiracy implemented by the New World Order against the Islāmic nation, within the framing theory, is amalgamation (uniting multiple entities into one). In this era, it is called globalization.

It is to blend truth with falsehood, good with evil, the pious with the wicked, *sunnah* with innovation, and the person of *sunnah* with the innovator. It is to combine the Qur'ān with the abrogated, distorted books like the Torah and the Gospel into one book. It is to combine the masjid and the church into one building. It is to unite the Muslim and the disbeliever and unify the religions.

The theory of amalgamation is the most lethal plot meant to disintegrate religion from the soul of the believer. It is designed to poison the Muslim community and shake their faith. It is meant to engross them in desires and immerse them in pleasures while dulling their senses until they do not recognize good or evil and some of them will gradually apostate from their religion.[1]

Translator's Addendum

———

Carl Harry Claudy (1879-1957)

Carl Harry Claudy, a freemason journalist for the New York Herald said, "In his private petitions, a man may petition God or Jehovah, Allāh or Buddha, Mohammed or Jesus; he may call upon the God of Israel or the Great First Cause. Masonry does not specify any god of any creed; she requires merely that you believe in some deity, give him what name you will ... any god will do ..."[2]

Freemason leader Albert Pike said, "Masonry (is that religion) around whose altars the Christian, Hebrew, Moslem, Brahman (Hindu), and followers of Confucius and Zoroaster, can assemble as brethren and unite in prayer ..."[3]

———

End of Translator's Addendum

---

[1] Invalidating the theory of mixing Islam with other religions.
[2] Carl Claudy, *Introduction to Freemasonry.*
[3] Albert Pike, "Morals and Dogma," 226, (1906).

DEVIANT SECTS PROMOTING THE AGENDA OF THE NEW WORLD ORDER'S UNITY OF RELIGION

BAHÁ'Í FAITH AND THE NEW WORLD ORDER

Bahá'í Faith is a deviant sect founded in 1863 by Mīrzā Ḥusayn 'Alī Nūrī who assumed the name Bahá'u'lláh. His followers consider him to be the Manifestation of God. Their fundamental principle is the unity of all religions and humanity, which they call the New World Order.

The term "new world order," in Bahá'í Faith, refers to the replacement of the collective political norms and values of the 19th century with a new system of worldwide governance that incorporates the Bahá'í ideals of unity and justice for all nations, races, creeds, and classes. The idea of world unification, both politically and spiritually, is at the heart of Bahá'í Faith teachings.[1]

---

[1] *Encyclopedia of Global Religion*, SAGE Publications.

Shoghí Effendi (1897-1957)

He was the head of Bahá'í Faith from 1921 until his death and described the new world order as the "world's future super-state with Bahá'í Faith as the State Religion of an independent and Sovereign Power."[1]

Shoghí Effendi said, "The point is not that there is something intrinsically wrong with Masonry, which no doubt has many very high ideals and principles and has had a very good influence in the past. The reasons why the guardian feels that it is imperative for the Bahá'ís to be dissociated from Masonry at this time, and I might add, other secret associations, is that we are the building blocks of Bahá'u'lláh's New World Order."[2]

Some of the principles outlined in their new world order include:[3]

∴ The unity of all religions.

∴ Universal peace based on global collective security.

∴ One world government with an elected world parliament and a universal law code for all nations.

∴ A world tribunal, world police force, and universal bill of human rights.

∴ A world currency.

∴ An auxiliary universal language.

---

[1] "Local and National Houses of Justice," *The World Order of Bahá'u'lláh*, Bahá'í Publishing Trust.
[2] Shoghi Effendi, *Lights of Guidance*, 422.
[3] Stanwood Cobb, *The Unity of Nation*.

Bahá'í Faith teaches that the world should adopt an international auxiliary language that people would use in addition to their mother tongue. The auxiliary language of choice is the Esperanto language created by Polish ophthalmologist L. L. Zamenhof in 1887. His daughter, Lidia Zamenhof, became a member of Bahá'í Faith in 1925.[1] She was murdered at the Treblinka extermination camp during the Holocaust.

Baha'u'llah said, "Now praise be to God that Dr. Zamenhof has invented the Esperanto language. It has all the potential qualities of becoming the international means of communication. All of us must be grateful and thankful to him for this noble effort; for in this way, he has served his fellowmen well. With untiring effort and self-sacrifice on the part of its devotees, Esperanto will become universal. Therefore, every one of us must study this language and spread it as far as possible."[2]

EFFORTS TO PROMOTE ESPERANTO AS THE UNIVERSAL LANGUAGE

Online: Wikipedia has over 286,000 articles in Esperanto. On February 22, 2012, Google Translate added Esperanto as its 64th language. On May 28, 2015, the language learning platform Duolingo launched a free Esperanto course for English speakers.

Government: The Chinese government has used Esperanto since 2001 for daily news on its website china.org.cn. Vatican Radio has an

---

[1] *A Concise Encyclopedia of Bahá'í Faith*, Oxford.
[2] Dr. John Esslemont, *Bahá'u'lláh and the New Era*, 2006 ed. (2006), 182.

Esperanto version of its website. The U.S. Army published military phrasebooks in Esperanto from the 1950s until the 1970s for use in war games.[1]

Popular Culture: Esperanto has been used in movies and television dating back to the 1920s. Idiot's Delight, released in 1939, features locals of an unidentified European country speaking Esperanto. The lead in this movie was actor Clark Gable, referred to as the King of Hollywood. He was a freemason belonging to Beverly Hills Lodge No. 528 in California.[2]

Road to Singapore, released in 1940, starring Bing Crosby and Bob Hope, features a song with Esperanto lyrics. In modern times, the 1994 film Street Fighter, featuring actor Jean-Claude Van Damme, has street signs and labels written in Esperanto. Esperanto is the second language spoken in the movie Blade: Trinity starring actor Wesley Snipes.

Esperanto is also used in video games and children's television programs. The opening song to the popular video game Final Fantasy XI, Memoro de la Ŝtono, was written in Esperanto. The composer, Nobuo Uematsu, felt that Esperanto was a good language to symbolize worldwide unity. Esperanto is available in the language selection in the video game Minecraft. In the animated action-adventure television series Danny Phantom, featured on Nickelodeon, the character Wulf spoke Esperanto in episode 15.

---

[1] *The Universal Language.* Directed by Sam Green. 2011.
[2] *Royal Arch Mason Magazine*, Spring 1981, 271

AHMADIYYA, FOUNDED BY GHULĀM AHMAD

Shaykh Muḥammad ibn ʿAbdullāh ibn Subail (☙) said:

It is not hidden to any Muslim the efforts the colonialists have made to block the Muslims from their religion and distance them from it, due to their hostility and hatred for Islām and the Muslims. From the efforts of the British colonialists to impede the Muslims from their religion is their sending a man who claimed prophecy, the man named Ghulām Aḥmad Mīrzā. If it was said about him that he was a prophet for Britain, its messenger and propagandist, this statement would be correct. He praised and commended the virtue of Britain over everyone else. He propagandized it and opposed the Muslims in defense of Britain.[1]

Translator's Addendum

_____

The Ahmadiyya sect established a missionary office in Haifa, Israel. It is one of the largest missionary centers in the world and includes a mosque, house for evangelization, public library, bookstore, and school. This office publishes a monthly magazine called *Al-Bushra*. The phrase "al-Bushra" is used by Christian evangelists and it means to deliver good news or evangelize. The Ahmadiyya community was first established in this region in the 1920s in what was then the British Mandate of Palestine.

_____

End of Translator's Addendum

_____

[1] *The Clear Clarification in Exposing the Qadiyani Ahmadiyya Sect.*

ORGANIZATIONS PROMOTING THE AGENDA OF THE NEW WORLD ORDER'S UNITY OF RELIGION

COEXIST FOUNDATION

Polish graphic designer Piotr Mlodozeniec created the first coexist design incorporating only three religions—Judaism, Christianity, and Islām—for an art competition held by the Museum on the Seam in Jerusalem.

The Coexist Foundation President, Dr. Tarek Elgawhary, purchased the trademark rights for the sticker and now it is sold on their website to raise money to promote unity among religions. The original design has been changed and manipulated many times to include various religions.

The bumper sticker spells "COEXIST" using a crescent moon for the letter C to represent Islām. A peace sign is used for the letter O to represent Pacifism. The Hindu Om symbol is used for the letter E to represent Hinduism. The star of David is used for the letter X to represent Judaism. A pentagram is used to for the dot atop the letter I to represent

Wicca or pagan witchcraft. A yin-yang symbol is used for the letter S to represent Taoism. A cross is used for the letter T to represent Christianity. The letters are often portrayed in rainbow colors to represent the LGBTQ community.

The Coexist Foundation partnered with Cambridge's Inter-Faith Programme with plans to establish the Abraham House, a place where people come together to learn about Judaism, Christianity, and Islām in a unique environment. Currently, the Coexist Foundation supports Cambridge's Inter-Faith Programme called In Scriptural Reasoning. Participants meet to read passages from their respective sacred texts. The goal is not agreement, but rather growth in understanding one another's traditions and deeper exploration of the texts and their possible interpretations.

THE HIGHER COMMITTEE OF HUMAN FRATERNITY

The Higher Committee of Human Fraternity is currently comprised of nine members: five Muslims; one Jewish rabbi; two Catholics, members of the Roman Curia;[1] and one United Nations official with no stated religion in her biography. Since its formation, the committee has met twice at the Vatican and once at the United Nations headquarters in New York.

---

[1] Those who assist the Pope in governing the Catholic Church.

The first initiative of the committee is to the Abrahamic Family House, set to be completed in 2022. It will be an interfaith complex in Abu Dhabi that will unite a church, a synagogue, and a mosque.

UNESCO (UNITED NATIONS EDUCATIONAL, SCIENTIFIC AND CULTURAL ORGANIZATION)

Shaykh 'Abdul Muḥsin al-Badr said:

The worst westernization in this country is what happened with the Higher Education Council in terms of creating law schools and Sharī'ah law colleges because these types of colleges are presented to countries that submit to man-made laws. As for the country of Saudi, to institute these laws here would be from the greatest of evil and falsehood. The difference between Sharī'ah law and man-made laws is like the difference between the Creator and the creation. Some of the scholars have clarified the vast difference between the laws invented by man and the laws sent down by Allāh (﷾). From the worst forms of westernization was the approval of the Higher Education Council to recommend forming a committee to study the possibility of benefiting from UNESCO Scientific Chairs, and the subsequent approval of twelve chairs beneath the umbrella of UNESCO. These include the UNESCO Chair for Interfaith and Intercultural Dialogue, the UNESCO Chair for Community Media, the UNESCO Chair for Quality in Higher Education at Imām Muḥammad bin Saūd Islāmic University, and the UNESCO Chair in the field of education for sustainable development in the Kingdom of Saudi Arabia at King Saūd University.

INDIVIDUALS PROMOTING THE AGENDA OF THE NEW WORLD ORDER'S UNITY OF RELIGION

Roger Garaudy (1913-2012)

Roger Garaudy was a French philosopher and communist author who purportedly converted to Islām in 1982.

Shaykh 'Abdul 'Azīz ibn Baz wrote about him saying:

All praises belong to Allāh alone. May Allāh exalt the rank and send peace upon the final Prophet and upon his family, his companions collectively. As to what follows:

Recently there has been much conversation in the newspapers and magazines concerning the man named Roger Garaudy, the French communist who claimed he embraced Islām with love and conviction. Some Muslims were overjoyed with this news. They gave him a warm welcome, honored him, and they trusted him. They made him a member of the World Supreme Council of Mosques in the Muslim World League. He became a speaker and debater at seminars and lectures in the Muslim world. Then his reality was unveiled, and his reality became clear. That which he was hiding in his chest from hatred of Islām and the Muslims became manifest. He remained upon his disbelief and apostasy. He resembled the hypocrites, those described by Allāh (ﷻ) in His statement,

$$﴿ وَإِذَا لَقُوكُمْ قَالُوا آمَنَّا وَإِذَا خَلَوْا عَضُّوا عَلَيْكُمُ الْأَنَامِلَ مِنَ الْغَيْظِ ۚ ﴿١١٩﴾ ﴾$$

And when they meet you, they say, "We believe." But when they are alone, they bite the tips of their fingers at you in rage.[1]

In his final interview with *The Majalla* magazine in issue 839, he informed them that he did not abandon his initial beliefs nor did he embrace the Islām that the Muslims are upon. Rather, he embraced a form of Islām that he envisioned within his own mind. He claimed Islām was a mixture of religions comprised of Judaism and Christianity. He said the Islām that he envisioned was the true Islām, not the Islām that Allāh (﷾) sent Muḥammad (ﷺ) with. He said the Islām that he envisioned is the religion of Ibrāhīm (ﷺ). He said Ibrāhīm was the first Muslim and Islām began with Ibrāhīm. But Ibrāhīm (ﷺ) was not a Jew, Christian, or Muslim with the Islām that the Muslims are upon today. Garaudy is a liar. For indeed, Islām is to single out Allāh (﷾), alone, in worship while abandoning everything that is worshipped other than Him. And this existed before Ibrāhīm. This has existed since the time of Adam (ﷺ), Nuh (ﷺ), and all the prophets and messengers. This is the religion that Allāh (﷾) sent our Prophet Muḥammad (ﷺ) with. Allāh (﷾) said,

$$﴿ ثُمَّ أَوْحَيْنَا إِلَيْكَ أَنِ اتَّبِعْ مِلَّةَ إِبْرَاهِيمَ حَنِيفًا ۖ وَمَا كَانَ مِنَ الْمُشْرِكِينَ ۝١٢٣ ﴾$$

---

[1] Sūrah 'Āli 'Imrān 3:119.

Then We revealed to you, (O Muḥammad), to follow the religion of Abraham, inclining toward
truth; and he was not of those who associated partners with Allāh.[1]

This is the religion of the Muslims today, those that follow
Muḥammad (ﷺ). Allāh (ﷻ) said,

$$﴿ إِنَّ الدِّينَ عِندَ اللَّهِ الْإِسْلَامُ ١٩ ﴾$$

Indeed, the religion in the sight of Allāh is Islām.[2]

The religion of Ibrāhīm (ﷺ) was not a mixture of truth and falsehood as
this misguided man claimed; rather, his religion was pure unadulterated
monotheism for Allāh (ﷻ), free from all forms of polytheism and free
from the people of polytheism. Allāh (ﷻ) said,

$$﴿ قَدْ كَانَتْ لَكُمْ أُسْوَةٌ حَسَنَةٌ فِي إِبْرَاهِيمَ وَالَّذِينَ مَعَهُ إِذْ$$

$$قَالُوا لِقَوْمِهِمْ إِنَّا بُرَآءُ مِنكُمْ وَمِمَّا تَعْبُدُونَ مِن دُونِ اللَّهِ$$

$$كَفَرْنَا بِكُمْ وَبَدَا بَيْنَنَا وَبَيْنَكُمُ الْعَدَاوَةُ وَالْبَغْضَاءُ أَبَدًا حَتَّىٰ$$

$$تُؤْمِنُوا بِاللَّهِ وَحْدَهُ ٤ ﴾$$

---

[1] Sūrah an-Naḥl 16:123.
[2] Sūrah 'Āli 'Imrān 3:19.

> Indeed, there has been an excellent example for you in Ibrāhīm and those with him, when they said to their people: "Verily, we are free from you and whatever you worship besides Allāh, we have rejected you, and there has started between us and you hostility and hatred forever, until you believe in Allāh Alone.[1]

This misguided individual believes that to disassociate from disbelief, polytheism, and the idolatry of the Jews and Christians causes division because Islām—in his mind—is to unite between the Muslim and non-Muslim. He wants Islām to unite two opposites. And he declares the Muslims who disagree with him to be disbelievers.

He stated, "My greatest pride is to have remained faithful to my dream as a 20-year-old, the unity of the three religions, Christianity, Judaism, and Islām."

The judgment upon Roger Garaudy is not as an apostate from the religion of Islām. Rather, he is a disbeliever who never entered the religion at all, as stated in his own words. He said, "I converted to Islām without abandoning my own beliefs and intellectual convictions."[2]

---

[1] Sūrah al-Mumtaḥanah 60:4.
[2] "The Ruling on Roger Garaudy and His Interview with the Majalla Magazine".

Sayyid Qutb (1906-1966)

Shaykh Rabee' said:[1]

Sayyid Qutb said, "The Islāmic community is a global society, meaning that it is a community that is not based upon race, nationality, or geographic location. It is a society open to all human beings without regard to gender, color, or language. Rather, it does not even look at religion or creed.[2] Sayyid Qutb said, "I often went to church and listened to preachers in the church, and the music, chants, and prayers. And I often listened to the fathers' broadcasts on radio stations during Christian holidays."

I say this is the universal Masonic call. The apparent call is to universal humanity while the hidden agenda is to achieve the goal of the Zionists.

Sayyid Qutb said, "Islām does not want freedom of worship for its followers alone, but rather establishes this right for the followers of different religions, and obliges Muslims to defend this right for everyone, and authorizes them to fight for the right, the right of guaranteeing freedom for all religious people. . . In this way, it realizes that this is a free world in which everyone can live in peace, enjoying their religious freedoms on an equal footing with Muslims and with the protection of Muslims."[3]

---

[1] *The Catastrophe Within the Books of Sayyid Qutb.*
[2] *Towards an Islamic Society*, 92-93.
[3] *Towards an Islamic Society*, 106.

I say Islām does not suffice with freedom of worship for the Muslims; rather, it continues to invite non-Muslims to embrace Islām. When the Muslim society was at full strength and they were free to worship Allāh, the Messenger of Allāh (ﷺ) wrote letters to the kings of the world inviting them to embrace Islām. He wrote a letter to Caesar, the king of Rome, inviting him to embrace Islām. He wrote to him saying, "Embrace Islām and you will have security. Allāh will reward you two-fold. But if you reject, you will incur the sin of your subjects that follow you." He wrote letters to the non-Muslim leaders inviting them to Islām with the Qur'ānic verse,

$$ ﴿ يَا أَهْلَ الْكِتَابِ تَعَالَوْا إِلَىٰ كَلِمَةٍ سَوَاءٍ بَيْنَنَا وَبَيْنَكُمْ أَلَّا نَعْبُدَ إِلَّا اللَّهَ وَلَا نُشْرِكَ بِهِ شَيْئًا وَلَا يَتَّخِذَ بَعْضُنَا بَعْضًا أَرْبَابًا مِّن دُونِ اللَّهِ ﴿٦٤﴾ ﴾ $$

O people of the Scripture (Jews and Christians): Come to a word that is just between us and you, that we worship none but Allāh, and that we associate no partners with Him, and that none of us shall take others as lords besides Allāh.[1]

---

[1] Sūrah 'Āli 'Imrān 3:64.

RULING ON THE CALL TO UNIFY RELIGIONS

The Permanent Committee for Research and Verdicts[1] published a treatise entitled *The Invalidity of Uniting the Religions*. They stated:

All praises belong to Allāh, alone. May Allāh exalt the rank and send peace upon the final Prophet and upon his family, his companions, and those that follow him in goodness until the Day of Judgment. As to what follows, indeed the Standing Committee for Academic Research and Issuing Fatwas reviewed the questions received, as well as opinions and articles published in the media regarding the call for uniting the religions of Islām, Judaism, and Christianity. They also considered what would result from this call, such as building a masjid, church, and synagogue in one building and the call to print the Qur'ān, Torah, and New Testament beneath one book cover. Also, there would be the issue of various seminars and conferences being held by different societies in the East and the West. After reflecting and studying the issue, the following verdict is given.

First: It is from the fundamental beliefs in Islām which must be known by necessity, and the Muslims have agreed that there is no true religion upon the face of the earth other than the religion of Islām. It is the seal of all religions. It abrogates all religions, ideologies, and legislations that came before it. Consequently, there is no religion upon the face of the earth by which Allāh (﷾) can be worship with other than Islām. Allāh (﷾) said,

---

[1] Members who signed this fatwa include Shaykh bin Baz, Shaykh ʿAbdul Azīz ʿAlī Shaykh, and Shaykh Fawzān.

﴿ وَمَن يَبْتَغِ غَيْرَ الْإِسْلَامِ دِينًا فَلَن يُقْبَلَ مِنْهُ وَهُوَ فِي

الْآخِرَةِ مِنَ الْخَاسِرِينَ ﴿٨٥﴾ ﴾

And whoever seeks a religion other than Islām, it will never be accepted of him, and in the Hereafter, he will be one of the losers.[1]

Second: It is from the fundamental principles of Islām that the Book of Allāh (﷾), the Noble Qur'ān, is the final Book sent down from the Lord of all that exists. It abrogates all books revealed before it, to include the Torah, the New Testament (Gospel), and other books. It is, likewise, superior to all other books. Therefore, there is no book by which Allāh (﷾) can be worshipped by other than the Noble Qur'ān. Allāh (﷾) said,

﴿ وَأَنزَلْنَا إِلَيْكَ الْكِتَابَ بِالْحَقِّ مُصَدِّقًا لِّمَا بَيْنَ يَدَيْهِ مِنَ

الْكِتَابِ وَمُهَيْمِنًا عَلَيْهِ ۖ فَاحْكُم بَيْنَهُم بِمَا أَنزَلَ اللَّهُ ۖ وَلَا تَتَّبِعْ

أَهْوَاءَهُمْ عَمَّا جَاءَكَ مِنَ الْحَقِّ ﴿٤٨﴾ ﴾

And We have revealed to you, (O Muḥammad), the Book in truth, confirming that which preceded it of the Scripture and as a criterion over it. So,

---

[1] Sūrah 'Āli 'Imrān 3:85.

judge between them by what Allāh has revealed and do not follow their inclinations away from what has come to you of the truth.[1]

Third: It is obligatory to believe that the Torah and the New Testament (Gospel) have been abrogated by the Noble Qur'ān, and both of them have been altered and changed with additions and subtractions. Allāh (ﷻ) said,

$$\text{﴿ فَبِمَا نَقْضِهِم مِّيثَاقَهُمْ لَعَنَّاهُمْ وَجَعَلْنَا قُلُوبَهُمْ قَاسِيَةً ۖ}$$

$$\text{يُحَرِّفُونَ الْكَلِمَ عَن مَّوَاضِعِهِ ۙ وَنَسُوا حَظًّا مِّمَّا ذُكِّرُوا بِهِ ۚ}$$

$$\text{وَلَا تَزَالُ تَطَّلِعُ عَلَىٰ خَائِنَةٍ مِّنْهُمْ إِلَّا قَلِيلًا مِّنْهُمْ ﴿١٣﴾ ﴾}$$

So, because of their breach of the covenant, We cursed them and made their hearts grow hard. They change the words from their (right) places and have abandoned a good part of the Message that was sent to them. And you will not cease to discover deceit in them, except a few of them.[2]

---

[1] Sūrah al-Mā'idah 5:48.
[2] Sūrah al-Mā'idah 5:13.

And Allāh (﷾) said,

$$﴾ فَوَيْلٌ لِّلَّذِينَ يَكْتُبُونَ الْكِتَابَ بِأَيْدِيهِمْ ثُمَّ يَقُولُونَ هَذَا مِنْ عِندِ اللَّهِ لِيَشْتَرُوا بِهِ ثَمَنًا قَلِيلًا ۖ فَوَيْلٌ لَّهُم مِّمَّا كَتَبَتْ أَيْدِيهِمْ وَوَيْلٌ لَّهُم مِّمَّا يَكْسِبُونَ ﴿٧٩﴾ ﴿$$

Then woe to those who write the Book with their own hands and then say, "This is from Allāh," to purchase with it a little price! Woe to them for what their hands have written and woe to them for that they earn thereby.[1]

And Allāh (﷾) said,

$$﴾ وَإِنَّ مِنْهُمْ لَفَرِيقًا يَلْوُونَ أَلْسِنَتَهُم بِالْكِتَابِ لِتَحْسَبُوهُ مِنَ الْكِتَابِ وَمَا هُوَ مِنَ الْكِتَابِ وَيَقُولُونَ هُوَ مِنْ عِندِ اللَّهِ وَمَا هُوَ مِنْ عِندِ اللَّهِ وَيَقُولُونَ عَلَى اللَّهِ الْكَذِبَ وَهُمْ يَعْلَمُونَ ﴿٧٨﴾ ﴿$$

And verily, among them is a party who distort the Book with their tongues, so that you may think it

---

[1] Sūrah al-Baqarah 2:79.

is from the Book, but it is not from the Book, and they say: "This is from Allāh," but it is not from Allāh; and they speak a lie against Allāh while they know it.[1]

Whatever from these books that was authentic has been abrogated by Islām. Everything other than that, then it is altered or distorted. The Prophet (ﷺ) became angry when he saw 'Umār ibn al-Khaṭṭāb with a page containing words from the Torah. The Prophet (ﷺ) said,

أَمُتَهَوِّكُونَ فِيهَا يَا ابْنَ الْخَطَّابِ ، وَالَّذِي نَفْسِي بِيَدِهِ ، لَقَدْ جِئْتُكُمْ بِهَا بَيْضَاءَ نَقِيَّةً

Are you confused, O son of al-Khaṭṭāb? By the One in Whose Hand is my soul, I have brought it (the message of Islām) to you clear and pure.[2]

Fourth: From the fundamental beliefs in Islām is that our Prophet and Messenger Muḥammad (ﷺ) is the seal of the prophets and messengers. As Allāh (ﷻ) said,

﴿ مَّا كَانَ مُحَمَّدٌ أَبَا أَحَدٍ مِّن رِّجَالِكُمْ وَلَكِن رَّسُولَ اللَّهِ وَخَاتَمَ النَّبِيِّينَ ۗ وَكَانَ اللَّهُ بِكُلِّ شَيْءٍ عَلِيمًا ﴾

---

[1] Sūrah 'Āli 'Imrān 3:78.
[2] Aḥmad 14736, classed as ḥasan by al-Albānī in *Irwa al-Ghaleel*, 6/34.

Muḥammad is not the father of any man among you, but he is the Messenger of Allāh and the last of the prophets. And Allāh is Ever All-Aware of everything.[1]

Thus, there does not remain any messenger whom it is obligatory to follow other than Muḥammad (ﷺ). Even if there were a prophet or messenger of Allāh (ﷻ) still alive, he would have to follow Prophet Muḥammad (ﷺ). As Allāh (ﷻ) said,

﴿ وَإِذْ أَخَذَ اللَّهُ مِيثَاقَ النَّبِيِّينَ لَمَا آتَيْتُكُم مِّن كِتَابٍ وَحِكْمَةٍ

ثُمَّ جَاءَكُمْ رَسُولٌ مُّصَدِّقٌ لِّمَا مَعَكُمْ لَتُؤْمِنُنَّ بِهِ وَلَتَنصُرُنَّهُ ۚ

قَالَ أَأَقْرَرْتُمْ وَأَخَذْتُمْ عَلَىٰ ذَٰلِكُمْ إِصْرِي ۖ قَالُوا أَقْرَرْنَا ۚ قَالَ

فَاشْهَدُوا وَأَنَا مَعَكُم مِّنَ الشَّاهِدِينَ ﴿٨١﴾ ﴾

And (remember) when Allāh took the covenant of the prophets, saying: "Take whatever I gave you from the Book and wisdom, and afterwards there will come to you a Messenger (Muḥammad) confirming what is with you. You must, then, believe in him and help him." Allāh said: "Do you agree (to it) and will you take up My Covenant?" They said:

---

[1] Sūrah al-'Aḥzāb 33:40.

"We agree." He said: "Then bear witness; and I am with you among the witnesses (for this)."[1]

Jesus, the Prophet of Allāh (ﷻ), when he descends during the final days, he will be a follower of Muḥammad (ﷺ). He will judge by his legislation. Allāh (ﷻ) said,

$$\text{﴿ الَّذِينَ يَتَّبِعُونَ الرَّسُولَ النَّبِيَّ الْأُمِّيَّ الَّذِي يَجِدُونَهُ مَكْتُوبًا}$$

$$\text{عِندَهُمْ فِي التَّوْرَاةِ وَالْإِنجِيلِ ﴿١٥٧﴾ ﴾}$$

Those who follow the Messenger, the unlettered prophet, whom they find written in what they have of the Torah and the Gospel.[2]

It is also from the fundamental beliefs of Islām that Muḥammad (ﷺ) was sent to all of mankind collectively. Allāh (ﷻ) said,

$$\text{﴿ وَمَا أَرْسَلْنَاكَ إِلَّا كَافَّةً لِّلنَّاسِ بَشِيرًا وَنَذِيرًا وَلَٰكِنَّ أَكْثَرَ}$$

$$\text{النَّاسِ لَا يَعْلَمُونَ ﴿٢٨﴾ ﴾}$$

---

[1] Sūrah 'Āli 'Imrān 3:81.
[2] Sūrah al-'A'rāf 7:157.

And We have not sent you (O Muḥammad) except as a giver of glad tidings and a warner to all mankind, but most of men know not.[1]

And Allāh (ﷻ) said,

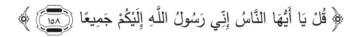

﴿ قُلْ يَا أَيُّهَا النَّاسُ إِنِّي رَسُولُ اللَّهِ إِلَيْكُمْ جَمِيعًا ﴾

Say, (O Muḥammad), "O mankind, indeed I am the Messenger of Allāh to you all."[2]

Fifth: It is from the fundamental beliefs of Islām that it is obligatory to believe that everyone who does not enter into Islām is a disbeliever, to include the Jews, Christians, and other than them. And they are called disbelievers. If they die upon that they will be in the Hellfire. Allāh (ﷻ) said,

﴿ لَمْ يَكُنِ الَّذِينَ كَفَرُوا مِنْ أَهْلِ الْكِتَابِ وَالْمُشْرِكِينَ مُنفَكِّينَ

حَتَّى تَأْتِيَهُمُ الْبَيِّنَةُ ﴾

Those who disbelieve from among the people of the Scripture (Jews and Christians) and among the

---

[1] Sūrah Saba' 34:28.
[2] Sūrah al-'A`rāf 7:158.

pagans, were not going to leave (their disbelief) until there came to them clear evidence.[1]

Allāh (ﷻ) said,

$$ ﴿ إِنَّ الَّذِينَ كَفَرُوا مِنْ أَهْلِ الْكِتَابِ وَالْمُشْرِكِينَ فِي نَارِ جَهَنَّمَ خَالِدِينَ فِيهَا ۚ أُولَٰئِكَ هُمْ شَرُّ الْبَرِيَّةِ ۝ ﴾ $$

Indeed, they who disbelieved among the people of the Scripture and the polytheists will be in the fire of Hell, abiding eternally therein. Those are the worst of creatures.[2]

The Prophet (ﷺ) said,

$$ وَالَّذِي نَفْسُ مُحَمَّدٍ بِيَدِهِ لَا يَسْمَعُ بِي أَحَدٌ مِنْ هَذِهِ الْأُمَّةِ يَهُودِيٌّ وَلَا نَصْرَانِيٌّ، ثُمَّ يَمُوتُ وَلَمْ يُؤْمِنْ بِالَّذِي أُرْسِلْتُ بِهِ إِلَا كَانَ مِنْ أَصْحَابِ النَّارِ $$

By Him in Whose Hand is the life of Muḥammad, he who amongst the community of Jews or Christians hears about me, but does not affirm his belief in that with which I have been sent and dies in this state (of disbelief), he shall be but one of the denizens of Hellfire.[3]

---

[1] Sūrah al-Bayyinah 98:1.
[2] Sūrah al-Bayyinah 98:6.
[3] *Saḥīḥ Muslim* 153.

For this reason, those who do not deem the Jews and Christians to be disbelievers, then he himself is a disbeliever. This is a principle within the legislation of Islām.

Sixth: Based upon these fundamental principles and facts from the legislation, the call to unity of religions, rapprochement between them, and blending them together is an evil, cunning call. The goal of this is to mix truth with falsehood. It is destructive to Islām and undermining to its foundations, and it drags its people into absolute apostasy. Allāh (ﷻ) said,

$$﴿ وَلَا يَزَالُونَ يُقَاتِلُونَكُمْ حَتَّىٰ يَرُدُّوكُمْ عَن دِينِكُمْ إِنِ اسْتَطَاعُوا ۚ ﴿٢١٧﴾ ﴾$$

And they will continue to fight you until they turn you back from your religion if they are able.[1]

And the statement of Allāh (ﷻ),

$$﴿ وَدُّوا لَوْ تَكْفُرُونَ كَمَا كَفَرُوا فَتَكُونُونَ سَوَاءً ۚ ﴿٨٩﴾ ﴾$$

They wish you would disbelieve as they disbelieved so you would become equal.[2]

---

[1] Sūrah al-Baqarah 2:217.
[2] Sūrah an-Nisā' 4:89.

Seventh: The effects of this call abolish the differences between Islām and disbelief, truth and falsehood, good and evil, and the Muslim and the disbeliever.

Eighth: If this call to unity of religion emanates from a Muslim, then this is considered clear apostasy from the religion of Islām because it collides with the fundamental principles of Islām. It is to be pleased with disbelief in Allāh (﷾). It invalidates the belief that the Noble Qur'ān abrogates all the books that came before it. It invalidates the belief that Islām abrogates all previous religions and legislations that came before it. Based on that, it is a religiously rejected idea, which is absolutely forbidden by all legal evidence in Islām from the Qur'ān, Sunnah, and consensus.

Ninth: Based upon what has proceeded, it is not permissible for the Muslim who believes in Allāh as his Lord, Islām as his religion, and Muḥammad (ﷺ) as his Prophet and Messenger to invite to this sinful call. It is not permissible to encourage the Muslims upon this, let alone to hold seminars and conferences promoting this.

It is not permissible for a Muslim to print the Torah or the New Testament (Gospel) as individual books. So how could it be permissible to print these books along with the Noble Qur'ān under one cover?! Whoever does this or calls to this is far astray. This is to combine the truth, which is the Noble Qur'ān, with the distorted abrogated books, the Torah and New Testament.

It is not permissible for the Muslim to answer the call to building a masjid, church, and synagogue in one building. To do so is to validate other religions as legitimate methods to worship Allāh (﷾). It is to deny that Islām is superior to all other religions. This is a call to three religions being equal and the people can select any of the three they desire. There is no doubt that affirming, believing, or being pleased with this is disbelief and misguidance because it opposes the clear text of the Noble Qur'ān, pure Sunnah, and consensus of the Muslims. This is to assert that the distortions from the Jews and Christians are actually from Allāh (ﷻ). And Allāh is far above such a thing. It is also not permissible to call churches houses of Allāh, or to say that the church-goers are worshipping Allāh within the church with worship that will be accepted by Allāh because they are worshipping with something other than Islām. Allāh (ﷻ) said,

$$\text{﴿ وَمَن يَبْتَغِ غَيْرَ الْإِسْلَامِ دِينًا فَلَن يُقْبَلَ مِنْهُ وَهُوَ فِي الْآخِرَةِ مِنَ الْخَاسِرِينَ (٨٥) ﴾}$$

And whoever seeks a religion other than Islām, it will never be accepted of him, and in the Hereafter, he will be one of the losers.[1]

Rather, they are houses in which they disbelieve in Allāh (ﷻ). We seek refuge with Allāh from disbelief and the disbelievers. Shaykh al-Islām ibn Taymiyyah (ﵫ) said in his collection of religious verdicts, "Synagogues and churches are not houses of Allāh, the only houses of Allāh are the masjids. Rather, they are houses in which Allāh is disbelieved in, even if they mentioned Him there. A house is only as good as its

---

[1] Sūrah 'Āli 'Imrān 3:85.

inhabitants, and the inhabitants of these homes are disbelievers. Thus, they are homes of the disbelievers."[1]

Tenth: From the obligatory matters which must be known is that it is obligatory upon the Muslims to invite the disbelievers, especially the Jews and Christians, to the religion of Islām with the clear text of the Book and the Sunnah.

But, this is done with clear preaching in the best manner without removing anything from the legislation of Islām. This is to convince them of the truth of Islām so they will enter it, or to establish the proof. Allāh (ﷻ) said,

$$﴿ قُلْ يَا أَهْلَ الْكِتَابِ تَعَالَوْا إِلَىٰ كَلِمَةٍ سَوَاءٍ بَيْنَنَا وَبَيْنَكُمْ أَلَّا نَعْبُدَ إِلَّا اللَّهَ وَلَا نُشْرِكَ بِهِ شَيْئًا وَلَا يَتَّخِذَ بَعْضُنَا بَعْضًا أَرْبَابًا مِّن دُونِ اللَّهِ ۚ فَإِن تَوَلَّوْا فَقُولُوا اشْهَدُوا بِأَنَّا مُسْلِمُونَ ﴿٦٤﴾ ﴾$$

Say (O Muḥammad): "O people of the Scripture (Jews and Christians): Come to a word that is just between us and you, that we worship none but Allāh, and that we associate no partners with Him, and that none of us shall take others as lords besides

---

[1] *Collection of Religious Verdicts*, 22 /162.

Allāh." Then, if they turn away, say: "Bear witness
that we are Muslims."[1]

As for meeting with them in order to please their desires and fulfill their
objectives while breaking the bonds of Islām and faith, this is falsehood
forbidden by Allāh (ﷻ), His Messenger (ﷺ), and the believers. And with
Allāh aid is sought for what they do.

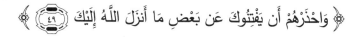

Beware of them, lest they tempt you away from
some of what Allāh has revealed to you.[2]

And with Allāh (ﷻ) lies all success. May Allāh exalt the rank of our
Prophet Muḥammad, his family, and his companions collectively.[3]

---

[1] Sūrah 'Āli 'Imrān 3:63.
[2] Sūrah al-Mā'idah 5:49.
[3] *The Invalidity of Uniting the Religions.*

THE MISSIONARIES

By Shaykh 'Abū Amar 'Alī Al Hudhayfī

Chapter One

THE REALITY OF CHRISTIANIZATION

The Definition of Christianization

Ibn Muthar[1] mention in his book *Lisān al-'Arab*, "Christianization is to enter Christianity." Likewise, the definition can be found in the authentic narration where the Prophet (ﷺ) said:

مَا مِنْ مَوْلُودٍ إِلاَّ يُولَدُ عَلَى الْفِطْرَةِ فَأَبَوَاهُ يُهَوِّدَانِهِ وَيُنَصِّرَانِهِ وَيُمَجِّسَانِهِ

Every child is born in a state of natural inclination (towards Islām), then his parents make him a Jew or a Christian or a Magian.[2]

---

[1] Ibn Muthar was a Libyan lexicographer of the Arabic language and author of a large dictionary called *Lisān al-'Arab* (The Tongue of the Arabs). He died in the year 1232 C.E., coinciding with 711 Hijri.

[2] From the *ḥadīth* of 'Abū Huraira, collected by *al-Bukhārī* (1358) and *Muslim* (2658).

We can say that Christianization is to enter some people into Christianity. And even if no one enters it, they are still diligent upon removing the people from their respective religions, especially the Muslims.

From this definition, we realize a number of issues.

One: This shows that the purpose of Christianization is not only to remove the Muslims from their religion but to remove others from their religions as well.

Two: The purpose of Christianization, at its core, is to enter the people into Christianity. If they are not able to do so, they will attempt to remove the people from their religion even if they have no religion at all after that.

* Pastor Samuel Marinus Zwemer,[1] one of the authors of *Dynamic Christianity and the World Today* said, "The task of the missionaries commissioned by the Christian countries to evangelize in the Islāmic countries is not to convert the Muslims to Christianity. This would be a guidance for them and an honor. Rather, your task is to remove the Muslims from Islām until they are a people with no connection to Allāh. This will result in them having no connection to the ethics and morals that the life of the Islāmic nation depends upon."

* In 1928 C.E. (1346 Hijri), the evangelism conference that took place on the Mount of Olives in Jerusalem—occupied

---

[1] Born in Vriesland, Michigan in 1867, nicknamed "the apostle to Islam," Zwemer was a member of the Arabian Mission from 1890 to 1913.

Palestine—was attended by 40 western Christian nations. During the conference, one of the speakers stood and said, "Do you think the goal of Christianization and its policy towards Islām is to remove the Muslims from their religion so they can become Christians?! If you believe this, then you are ignorant of Christianization and its goals. History has proven from long ago that the Muslim is unequivocally incapable of becoming Christian. Experience has shown us, and Christian politicians have shown us, that this is impossible. Rather, our only purpose is to remove the Muslim from Islām such that he will be confused about his religion and will have no system of belief by which he practices and utilizes for guidance and direction. At this point, he will be Muslim with nothing from Islām except the names, Aḥmad and Mustapha."

❖ In 1973 C.E. (1393 Hijri), there was a secret address delivered by Pope Shenouda in the church of St. Mark in Alexandria Egypt. During this address, he said, "It is essential to double the missionary efforts that are predicated upon the common goal of the next phase; that is to shift as many Muslims as possible away from their adherence to their religion, and it is not a necessity that they embrace Christianity. For surely, the goal is to destabilize religion in their souls and to cause the masses of them to question their Book and the validity of Muḥammad."

❖ Missionaries are not evangelists. Many people make the mistake of applying the term "evangelists" to the missionaries. This is because the missionaries have applied the name to themselves. Their objective for using this term is to mislead and deceive the poor who are unaware of the reality of this propaganda.

Translator's Addendum

Shaykh 'Abdul Ghanī 'Aoussāt said in his lecture "Warning against the dangers of Christianization," "Some Muslims mistakenly refer to the missionaries as evangelists. This is a mistake because in the Arabic language this word means to deliver good news that will make the people happy and bring them glad tidings. The Qur'ān states,

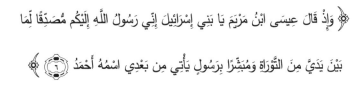

And (remember) when Jesus, son of Maryam, said: "O Children of Israel! I am the Messenger of Allāh unto you confirming the Torah which came before me, and a bringer of glad tidings of a Messenger to come after me, whose name shall be Aḥmad."[1]

Thus, the "evangelist," in the Arabic language (Mubashir), is the one who brings good news. They used the terminology to deceive the Muslims because the term evangelist in the Arabic language insinuates they are bringing good news to the people, while the reality is the opposite. Rather, it is the Muslims who deliver the good news of monotheism to the people. Therefore, we must use the term Christianization.

End of Translator's Addendum

---

[1] Sūrah aṣ-Ṣaf 61:6.

THE HATRED OF THE CHRISTIANS

The hearts of the Christians are filled with rage and hatred toward Islām and the Muslims. The reason for this hatred is because Allāh (🕮) has favored the believers with a clear light, an upright religion, and perfect guidance. Allāh (🕮) said:

$$﴿ مَّا يَوَدُّ الَّذِينَ كَفَرُوا مِنْ أَهْلِ الْكِتَابِ وَلَا الْمُشْرِكِينَ أَن يُنَزَّلَ عَلَيْكُم مِّنْ خَيْرٍ مِّن رَّبِّكُمْ ﴿١٠٥﴾ ﴾$$

Neither those who disbelieve among the people of the Scripture (Jews and Christians), nor the pagans, like that there should be sent down unto you any good from your Lord.[1]

And Allāh (🕮) said,

$$﴿ وَدَّ كَثِيرٌ مِّنْ أَهْلِ الْكِتَابِ لَوْ يَرُدُّونَكُم مِّن بَعْدِ إِيمَانِكُمْ كُفَّارًا حَسَدًا مِّنْ عِندِ أَنفُسِهِم مِّن بَعْدِ مَا تَبَيَّنَ لَهُمُ الْحَقُّ ﴿١٠٩﴾ ﴾$$

Many of the people of the Scripture (Jews and Christians) wish that they could turn you away as disbelievers after you have believed, out of envy

---

[1] Sūrah al-Baqarah 2:105.

from their own selves, even after the truth has become manifest unto them.[1]

And Allāh (ﷻ) said:

﴿ يَا أَيُّهَا الَّذِينَ آمَنُوا إِن تُطِيعُوا فَرِيقًا مِّنَ الَّذِينَ أُوتُوا الْكِتَابَ يَرُدُّوكُم بَعْدَ إِيمَانِكُمْ كَافِرِينَ ۝ وَكَيْفَ تَكْفُرُونَ وَأَنتُمْ تُتْلَىٰ عَلَيْكُمْ آيَاتُ اللَّهِ وَفِيكُمْ رَسُولُهُ ۗ وَمَن يَعْتَصِم بِاللَّهِ فَقَدْ هُدِيَ إِلَىٰ صِرَاطٍ مُّسْتَقِيمٍ ۝ ﴾

O you who believe! If you obey a group of those who were given the Scripture (Jews and Christians), they would (indeed) render you disbelievers after you have believed! And how could you disbelieve while to you are being recited the verses of Allāh and among you is His Messenger? And whoever holds firmly to Allāh has [indeed] been guided to a straight path.[2]

Allāh (ﷻ) said,

﴿ يَا أَيُّهَا الَّذِينَ آمَنُوا إِن تُطِيعُوا الَّذِينَ كَفَرُوا يَرُدُّوكُمْ عَلَىٰ أَعْقَابِكُمْ فَتَنقَلِبُوا خَاسِرِينَ ۝ ﴾

---

[1] Sūrah al-Baqarah 2:109.
[2] Sūrah 'Āli 'Imrān 3:100, 101.

O you who believe! If you obey those who disbelieve, they will send you back on your heels, and
you will turn back (from faith) as losers.[1]

Allāh (ﷻ) said,

﴿ وَدَّت طَّائِفَةٌ مِّنْ أَهْلِ الْكِتَابِ لَوْ يُضِلُّونَكُمْ وَمَا يُضِلُّونَ إِلَّا أَنفُسَهُمْ

وَمَا يَشْعُرُونَ ۩ ﴿٦٩﴾ ﴾

A party of the people of the Scripture (Jews and
Christians) wish to lead you astray. But they shall
not lead astray anyone except themselves, and they
perceive not.[2]

And Allāh (ﷻ) said,

﴿ قَدْ بَدَتِ الْبَغْضَاءُ مِنْ أَفْوَاهِهِمْ وَمَا تُخْفِي صُدُورُهُمْ أَكْبَرُ ۩ ﴿١١٨﴾ ﴾

Hatred has already appeared from their mouths, but
what their breasts conceal is far worse.[3]

---

[1] Sūrah 'Āli 'Imrān 3:149.
[2] Sūrah 'Āli 'Imrān 3:69.
[3] Sūrah 'Āli 'Imrān 3:118.

Allāh (ﷻ) said,

﴿ وَدَّ الَّذِينَ كَفَرُوا لَوْ تَغْفُلُونَ عَنْ أَسْلِحَتِكُمْ وَأَمْتِعَتِكُمْ فَيَمِيلُونَ عَلَيْكُم

مَّيْلَةً وَاحِدَةً ﴾ (١٠٢)

Those who disbelieve wish, if you were negligent of your arms and your baggage, to attack you in a single rush.[1]

Allāh (ﷻ) said,

﴿ وَيُرِيدُ الَّذِينَ يَتَّبِعُونَ الشَّهَوَاتِ أَن تَمِيلُوا مَيْلًا عَظِيمًا ﴾ (٢٧)

But those who follow their lusts wish that you (believers) should deviate tremendously away from the Right Path.[2]

Allāh (ﷻ) said,

﴿ وَلَن تَرْضَىٰ عَنكَ الْيَهُودُ وَلَا النَّصَارَىٰ حَتَّىٰ تَتَّبِعَ مِلَّتَهُمْ ﴾ (١٢٠)

---

[1] Sūrah an-Nisā' 4:102.
[2] Sūrah an-Nisā' 4:27.

> **Never will the Jews nor the Christians be pleased**
> **with you until you follow their religion.**[1]

This animosity will remain until Allāh (ﷻ) inherits the earth and those upon it, even if they display love for Islām and for the people as a whole.

THE HISTORY OF CHRISTIANIZATION

The Difference between Christianization and Evangelism

Christian evangelism has been around for long generations. It was not born during this era. Christianization is another matter, it is broader than evangelism. Its goals are much broader than the call to Christianity. In addition to evangelism, it aims to spread Christian supremacy over the entire world, or at least most of it. It aims to occupy the Islāmic lands, as well as other lands, and dominate them without the need for bloodshed, preventing the Muslims from raising the banner of *jihad* which will return honor to the Muslims by Allāh's permission. In addition to this, it has added a new facet. Christianization is no longer only the job of priests and monks; rather, today's missionaries include engineers, doctors, and other professionals from those who call to Christianity.

---

[1] Sūrah al-Baqarah 2:120.

STEALTH MODE AFTER EMERGENCE

In the beginning, they directed their efforts toward wars and fighting to eradicate Islām and wipe out the Muslims. But they noticed that Islām caused the Muslims to hold firmly to their religion and it brought about cohesion and solidity among them. Consequently, they resorted to the tactic of deception because this method harms the Muslims in a way the previous method did not. In the year 1920, the American Missionary Committee released a book that stated in the introduction, "From the most prominent matters connected to the United States entering World War I were the views and principles which were the objective of the missionaries that had been adopted by the American nation." Then they proclaimed that the purpose for joining the war was due to moral objectives, while these views and principles were now given political names.

The reality of Christianization is to colonize new lands under the guise of evangelism. And I did not find any words to explain this reality to the noble reader like the words of one of the Africans.[1] He said, "When the missionaries came to Africa, they had the Bible and we had the land. They said, 'Let us pray.' We closed our eyes. When we opened them, we had the Bible and they had the land."

---

[1] Translator's note: This statement was said by South African Anglican cleric Desmond Tutu.

Chapter Two

THE OBJECTIVES OF CHRISTIANIZATION

When we look at what has been written by the callers to Christianization concerning their goals and objectives, we find they have several objectives.

One: The elimination of Islām and its reality in the hearts of the Muslims

No doubt this is the initial goal as has been mentioned in the previous verses of Qur'ān. Thus, this is the main objective which precedes the other goals. The objective is to strip the Muslim of his religion and convert him to Christianity. And if he does not convert, then leave him with no religion. Both outcomes are agreeable.

The orientalist Chatelier[1] said, "If you want to war against Islām, break its spine and eliminate their doctrine which has prevailed over all

---

[1] Alfred Le Chatelier (1855-1929) was a French orientalist.

previous and subsequent creeds. Then, it is upon you to direct your destructive efforts toward the souls of the Muslim youth and the Islāmic nation by killing their religious pride with respect to their history and their Book, the Qur'ān."[1]

Pastor Zwemer, a leading missionary, said,[2] "Your task is to remove the Muslims from Islām until they are a people with no connection to Allāh. This will result in them having no connection to the ethics and morals which the life of the Islāmic nation depends upon. And by this work of yours, you will be vanguards of the colonization of the Islāmic world. You primed a generation in the Muslim lands that have no connection to Allāh, and they do not desire a connection to Him. You removed the Muslim from Islām and you did not convert him to Christianity; thus, the Muslim youth came ready to be colonized. They are not concerned with greatness. Their only concern in this world is to fulfill their desires. They love relaxation and laziness. If they study, they study to fulfill their desires. If they collect wealth, they collect wealth to fulfill their desires. If they hold a position in a center, it is only to fulfill their desires.[3]

---

[1] Chatelier went on to say, "You must utilize all possible means to turn them toward your culture and your history. Spread pornography amongst them and destroy their religious morals until all of them are heedless and gullible. (*The Conquest of the Muslim World*, page 264).

[2] This speech was delivered during a conference in Jerusalem during the year 1935 C.E.

[3] 'Abdur Razzāq Dayar Bakr, *Conquest of the Muslim.*

Two: Stopping the spread of Islām

They desire to stop the wave of Islām and slow the spread of Islām to the different regions and countries. They want to prevent other groups outside of Christianity from entering Islām, such as the Hindus and Buddhists. They desire to block the spread of Islām and spread Christianity in its place, or at the least allow the non-Christians to remain upon their belief systems (other than Islām).

John Garang[1] quoted a statement from a rebel crusader in Southern Sudan who said, "Sudan is the gateway of Islām and Arabism to Africa, so let our focus be to protect the key to this door so Islām and Arabism are not established in Sub-Saharan Africa."[2]

During a 1910 C.E. Christianization conference in Cairo, Gairdner[3] said, "We find ourselves faced with an Islāmic education and religious renaissance which requires us to move forward with our missionary work. We must keep in mind the gains we made in the past. For this reason, it is certainly the time to move forward with our work, wise planning, and implementation with a serious and intense mission among the Muslims in Syria and Palestine. We must draw the attention of all missionary groups currently working in this area to rush toward achieving this goal."

---

[1] John Garang (1945-2005) was a Sudanese politician and leader from 1983 to 2005.

[2] 'Abdul Wadūd Shalabi, *Crawling to Mecca*.

[3] William Henry Temple Gairdner (July 31, 1873 - May 22, 1928) was a British Christian missionary with the Church Missionary Society in Cairo, Egypt.

He also said, "And those students who are prepared to carry out proselytizing among Muslims must add to their programs the task of monitoring and studying the face of this new Islām in all its manifestations. This study can only take place in the Arab lands, and without question this place is Cairo.

Three: The destruction of the woman by advocating so-called women's rights

From their objective is the destruction of the woman by advocating so-called women's rights and concentrating on removing the Muslim woman from her home for two reasons. The first reason is this that results in the destruction of the community and corrupts morals and manners. The second reason is that if she answers their appeal and leaves the home, she is a quick means to transfer their propaganda to the Muslim family. This is because the woman is quickly affected by what she reads and hears.

For this reason, the missionaries give extra concern to propagating to the women. Rarely is there ever a Christianization conference without evangelizing to the Muslim women being one of the main topics of the seminar. This was witnessed during the pre-conference preparation for a seminar held in the U.S. state of Colorado in 1978 C.E.[1] One of the

---

[1] *The Glen Eyrie Report: Muslim Evangelization.*

topics[1] was "The Christian Approach to the Muslim Woman and Family."[2]

As for the Christianization conference held in Cairo in 1906 C.E., the participating female missionaries directed their efforts toward the following appeal: "There is no way for our mission to succeed except by bringing the Muslim women to Jesus. The number of Muslim women is extremely large, not less than 100 million. Thus, all of the glorious energy put forth to reach them must become greater than what has been done thus far."[3]

Four: Strengthening the non-Muslim minorities

From their objectives is to strengthen the non-Muslim minorities, especially the Christians among them. This is accomplished by shielding non-Muslims from all religions and ideologies except Christian ideology; expressly shielding them from Islām and financially empowering Christians. In Egypt for example, we find the Christian population is around 8% but they own close to 50% of the economy, with some sites reporting they own 70% in some sectors. For instance, Mobinil

---

[1] Translator's note: During the six months prior to the conference, 40 foundation papers were prepared by selected authors—men and women—to alert the participants to the complexity of issues related to the task before them. Ten papers were conceptual, in that they explored its major underlying postulates. Sixteen papers described key "givens" in the Christian encounter with Islam today. The final 14 papers defined concrete responses deemed essential to effective missionary service among Muslims. (Reference: Lausanne Movement).

[2] Written by Dr. Valerie J. Hoffman, Head Professor, Department of Religion, University of Illinois at Urbana.

[3] *Evangelization and Colonization*, 204.

Telecom,[1] in Egypt, is a Christian company and its directors are Christian. It is one of the corporations of Naguib Sawiris,[2] one of the largest financiers of Christianization in Egypt, who financed much of the missionary activities recognized by the missionaries themselves.

Five: Causing the Muslim to Question Islām

They desire for the Muslim to question Islām and to throw doubts in the hearts of the Muslims. This goal has been repeated in the attempts of the missionary known as Samuel Zwemer, who specialized in the practice of Christianization in the Arab lands in general, but especially the gulf region. He sent a letter to Chatelier in 1911 C.E. saying, "The issue that cannot not be disputed is that the success the missionaries had in changing the one who wanted to adopt the Islāmic creed and moral principles in the Ottoman lands, Qatr, Egypt and other places is much greater than the success western civilization had. We should not depend on baptism statistics to know the number of Muslims who officially converted to Christianity, because there are hundreds of whom Islām was snatched from their hearts and they embraced Christianity secretly.

Six: Controlling the Muslim population through birth control

---

[1] Currently known as Orange Egypt.
[2] Naguib Onsi Sawiris, born in 1954, is an Egyptian billionaire businessman, Chairman of Weather Investments' parent company, and Chairman of Orascom Telecom Media and Technology Holding S.A.E. Sawiris is an Egyptian Christian, following the teachings of the Coptic Orthodox Church.

From their plots is to control the Muslim population through birth control. For this reason, we find that everything connected to birth control—pills, condoms, and the like—are the cheapest items in the maternity clinics, and the World Health Organization is extremely generous in this arena.

Seven: Deporting Muslims to non-Muslims countries

They deport those they can to America, Canada, and other western countries, especially Somalia refugees or the youth who are fond of the West. They approach the youth from an angle which they love; thus, they are like ambassadors removing whoever they are able to remove.

Eight: Altering the school curriculum

They altered the school curriculum in the poor countries they reside in, or at least removed the Qur'ānic verses that speak of *jihad* in the path of Allāh (ﷻ) or those stating the people of the Book are disbelievers and the verses ordering Muslims to disavow them.

Nine: Sequestering the Muslim lands

From their goals is to seize the Muslim lands that were in their hands before the Muslims acquired them, such as Sham and other lands.

Translator's Addendum

Shaykh 'Abdul Ghanī 'Aoussāt said in his lecture "Warning Against the Dangers of Christianization," "When French troops took control of the city of Damascus in 1920, French general Henri Gouraud (1867-1946) stood at the grave of Ṣalāḥ ad-Dīn al-Ayyūbi (1137-1193) and said, 'Indeed we have returned, Ṣalāḥ ad-Dīn!'"

———

End of Translator's Addendum

Ten: Eliminate the Arabic language

They intend to eliminate the Arabic language because Arabic is the language of the Qur'ān.

Translator's Addendum

———

Shaykh 'Uthaymīn said, "Before the independence of Algeria, the French ruler said, 'We will not prevail over the Algerians as long as they read the Qur'ān and speak Arabic, so we must remove the Qur'ān from their presence and uproot Arabic from their tongues.'"[1]

———

End of Translator's Addendum

Eleven: Supporting the spread of corrupt ideology and morals in the Muslim lands

They give support toward spreading corrupt ideology and corrupt morals throughout the Muslim lands to bring about generations of Muslims who are deficient in knowledge and weak in religion. Thus, they control the media in order to control the minds of the Muslims. If they are able to Christianize a leader living in the midst of the Muslims so he can rule

---

[1] "Warning against the enemies of Islam," Friday sermon no. 12.

over them, they will surely do so. An example of this is Senghor,[1] the first president of Senegal.[2] He attended a Catholic boarding school[3] although his family, both his parents and his siblings, were all still Muslims. The Christians prepared him to rule over Senegal, which is 99% Muslim so he could war against the Muslims. After his affair was exposed, he was free to evangelize. A university bearing his name[4] was established to prepare missionaries in Muslim countries.

Twelve: Promoting freedom of opinion

They promote freedom of belief and opinion in order to divide the Muslims and keep them busy with these affairs.

Thirteen: Dissemination of Western ideas and doctrines

They disseminate Western ideology and thought. Chatelier said, "It is clear to us that the religious proselytism material which is backed by large amounts of money, the wisdom and mastermind behind this is to place Western thought throughout the Islāmic lands."

They have other dangerous goals as well, but these are the most dangerous, and they will have other goals as the days and nights pass.

---

[1] Léopold Sédar Senghor (October 9, 1906 – December 20, 2001).

[2] He held office from September 6, 1960 to December 31, 1980.

[3] At the age of eight, Senghor began his studies in Senegal, in the Ngasobil boarding school of the Fathers of the Holy Spirit. He was a Roman Catholic.

[4] Senghor University has campuses in Egypt; Morocco, Djibouti, Senegal, and other countries.

Chapter Three

MEANS AND METHODS

GENERAL MEANS OF CHRISTIANIZATION

The missionaries have many means of Christianization. Some say they have 700 methods or plans to evangelize. At face value its mercy, but its inner reality is punishment. They claim to do humanitarian work—building hospitals, treating the sick, building schools, and digging wells in rural areas—all under the pretext of humanitarian aid. While in reality, they come bearing a plot against Islām and the Muslims. We shall mention a few of these means in brief.

One: Medical treatment

Whenever these organizations hear of the poor or sick, they rush to their side, but it is not out of compassion. Rather, it is to convert them to Christianity.

Two: Exploiting disasters and unrest

These crusaders arrive during turmoil and war as saviors to convert the people to Christianity. David A. Fraser said, "In order for there to be change, a certain amount of crises and catastrophes are necessary to push the individuals and communities outside of their comfort zone. This may occur in the form of natural disasters, poverty, disease, and wars. It could come in the form of social ills such as apartheid or intolerance toward those of low social status.

Three: Military coups

They manage military coups believing their activity can increase with the fall of the governments. Thus, the missionary organizations have resorted to instigating military coups to achieve objectives Christianization was unable to achieve. Or, when they see the *dawah* to true Islām gaining strength, they attempt to overthrow the regime to put in place those who will promote Christianization. A missionary leaflet stated that the premier of northern Nigeria Aḥmadu Bello (؈) was the biggest obstacle in northern Nigeria against Christianization, and he was the one who opened the door for Islām in Nigeria.

Consequently, there was a coup d'état and Aḥmadu Bello was overthrown and assassinated.[1] The coup d'état major general, Johnson

---

[1] The 1966 Nigerian coup d'état began on January 15, 1966. Eleven senior Nigerian politicians, including Aḥmadu Bello, were assassinated.

Ironsi,[1] seized power. Ironsi grew up at the hands of the missionaries.[2] During the coup, students of the missionaries took positions of leadership. The military preparation of the Christians has been written about in some of the Egyptian books of Christianization. In these books, there is mention of Orthodox Christian militant organizations in Egypt, including the "Christian Jihad Group."

Four: Language institutes in Muslim lands

They establish foreign schools to teach various languages in the Muslim countries. Thus, they teach the Muslims English and use it as bait. And this bait is mixed with the call to pornography and Christian morals. There was a discussion titled "Current Status of Radio Broadcasting to Muslim Peoples," by Fred D. Acord[3] during the Christian conference in Colorado. He said, "English is essential for every Arab who wants to continue his studies or has hopes for immigration. We wrote to the BBC, as they have an excellent series of educational programs to teach English to native Arabic speakers. They authorized us to broadcast the

---

[1] Major General Johnson Thomas Umunnakwe Aguiyi-Ironsi (March 3, 1924 – July 29, 1966) seized power following the 1966 military coup, serving as the Nigerian Head of State from January 16, 1966 until his murder on July 29, 1966 by a group of mutinous northern army soldiers who revolted against his government in what was known as the July Counter Coup.

[2] He was a member of the Anglican Church. Anglicanism is a denomination within the Christian religion. It is made up of the Church of England and the Anglican Communion.

[3] Fredrick "Bud" Acord died on Aug. 4, 2014. He was in ministry for over 65 years. He served in Sudan, Ethiopia, Aden, and Lebanon, where he started a radio program called "Voice of Forgiveness," before moving back to America to represent the Sudan Interior Mission.

program through our radio and we have already made improvements to the series. At the conclusion of each program, we bait the listeners by asking the question, 'Who would like a free copy of a book containing English and Arabic side by side?' Then we send them a copy of the Bible in Arabic and English."

They transmit this broadcast to the people through their radio station in order to give Christianity to the people. We seek refuge in Allāh (﷾) from this plot.

Chatelier responded to the previously mentioned letter of Zwemer by saying, "There is no doubt that the Protestant and Catholic evangelists are unable to dislodge the Islāmic faith from the hearts of its adherents. This can only occur by broadcasting ideas that seep into the hearts by way of the European languages, such as English, German, Dutch, and French. Thus, Islām is wiped away by European newspapers and a path is laid to present Islāmic material so the missionaries can destroy the Islāmic ideology which preserves its strength and power.

Orientalist Gibb[1] said, "Education is the greatest suitable tool to use against Occidentalism.[2] The spread of western-style education will combat the stream of Occidentalism."

Five: Scholarships

---

[1] Sir Hamilton Alexander Rosskeen Gibb (January 2, 1895 – October 22, 1971), born in Alexandria, Egypt, was a Scottish historian on Orientalism.

[2] Occidentalism refers to representations and stereotypes of people situated in western regions, especially western European countries and the United States. These stereotypes are usually from the Muslim world.

They take advantage of them by granting scholarships to Muslim students outside of Islāmic countries. Thus, you find a community of Muslim children receiving education in Europe and America while they have institutions within their own countries. And these students are exposed to a strong campaign of missionaries.

Six: Building churches

They build the largest number of churches in Islāmic countries, giving special attention to the appearance of these churches. They even build churches in places where no Christians live to set up places for evangelist work. Their goal is to build missions, schools, and western high-rise buildings with strange appearances to stimulate the emotion and imagination of the visitors. In the mind of the missionaries, this will bring non-Christians closer to Christianity.

Translator's Addendum

————

The English Language Congregation (ELC) is one of the seven congregations that make up the National Evangelical Church in the Kingdom of Bahrain (NEC) and traces its history to 1893 when Reverend Samuel Zwemer and his small team of missionaries from the Reformed Church in America arrived in Bahrain and established the first protestant church in the Arabian Gulf.

————

End of Translator's Addendum

Seven: Propagating Christianity by way of satellite channels and radio

They evangelize through the radio and satellite channels. Fred D. Acord said, "It seems that today the radio is one of the main means by which to reach the Muslims in the Middle East and the North African closed countries. The radio can penetrate their barriers, cross the seas, jump over the deserts, and infiltrate the closed Muslim communities."

They spent roughly 12 million dollars on radio broadcasts alone, as reported by *Dawah Magazine* in Saudi Arabia.

Eight: Relief Organizations

They exploit the people's need for treatment during calamities, disasters, and the poverty of many of these countries at a time when their governments are unable to do enough to sustain them. The "relief organizations" exploit the misfortunes of the people, their diseases and tragedies, to invite them to their misguidance. No nation is afflicted with catastrophe from wars, earthquakes, or floods except that the missionary groups are seen going to the disaster area to give the Christian doctrine to the needy, along with a little medicine, a bite to eat, and a piece of clothing. Don't think for a minute that the Christians scrambling to these disaster sites is out of mercy they have for the people. Rather, it is an opportunity to evangelize. And they present it as though it is from the grace of Jesus (﷽). According to one of the specialists in this field, the missionaries' budget in this area exceeds 80 billion dollars.

Nine: Vocational Education

They seize the opportunity to open vocational education around the globe. Penrose,[1] the president of the American University of Beirut—formerly called The Syrian Protestant College—said in 1948 C.E., "It has been proven that education is the most valuable way for American missionaries to take advantage of their quest to evangelize Syria and Lebanon. For this reason, it was decided that the president of the Protestant college would come from the Syrian missionary.

Ten: Women's liberation movement

They manipulate women's issues such as the freedom of the women while hurling accusations of violence against them. They utilize these issues to infiltrate the Muslims and use it as an opportunity to insult Islām.

Eleven: Mishandling the Noble Qur'ān

They mishandle the Noble Qur'ān to measure the Muslims' jealousy, and to divulge whether any of those who have converted to Christianity from Islām will become emotional. In 1999, an incident took place in the city of Ibb, Yemen at Jibla Baptist Hospital.[2] They ripped out pages

---

[1] Stephen B.L. Penrose, Jr. was the president of American University of Beirut from 1948 to 1954.

[2] Jibla Hospital is a Southern Baptist hospital that opened in Taiz, Yemen in 1964, then moved to Jibla three years later. The Southern Baptist missionary board said its 80-bed Jibla Hospital treats more than 40,000 patients annually, providing free care to those who cannot afford it. Its missionaries also taught English and clinical skills at a nearby nursing school according to the board. Al Lindholm, the Baptists

from the Qur'ān and placed them in filthy places. This was done by some of those who apostated from Islām and converted to Christianity, and they were spreading Christianity throughout Yemen under the guise of providing free or inexpensive medical services. The story ends when a man entered the hospital and murdered some American men and women.[1]

WEAPONIZING MEDICINE AGAINST THE MUSLIMS

Christianization campaigns use strange and malicious means which indicate their hatred. This shows they will use any means to achieve their goals. I will mention some of their plots in the field of medical treatment so the Muslims can be aware of them.

One: Maiming Muslim patients

They weaken the Muslim patients by amputating their limbs and giving them injuries which they cannot recover from. This is so the Muslims will be too weak to establish any type of *jihad* or *dawah* and their families will remain needy.

---

chief representative, said, "The hospital contains a chapel where Yemenis sometimes come to hear Bible stories and sing songs." Lindholm said, "Open evangelism, to me, is standing on the street corner selling Bibles. Do we evangelize? No. Are we asked questions about our faith almost daily? Yes, and we answer them as honestly as we know how." (Ian Fisher, *New York Times*, January 16, 2003).

[1] In 2002, a gunman allegedly shot three U.S. humanitarian workers dead and wounded a fourth at Jibla Hospital.

Two: Population control

They open "Motherhood and Children" centers and pass out millions of birth control pills and tens of thousands of cheap or free condoms to reduce the Muslim population.

Three: Caesarean childbirths

There has been a surprisingly large increase in cesarean births among the Muslims. Shaykh 'Uthaymīn was asked whether Muslim couples delaying pregnancy and using IUD (intrauterine device) birth control see a benefit in doing so. He responded by saying, "There is no doubt that using contraceptive pills and drugs is in opposition to the Islāmic legislation, and in contradiction to what the Prophet (ﷺ) desired for this 'ummah. The Prophet (ﷺ) wanted for this 'ummah to increase.

تَزَوَّجُوا الْوَدُودَ الْوَلُودَ فَإِنِّي مُكَاثِرٌ بِكُمُ الأُمَمَ

Marry the one who is loving and fertile, for I will be proud of your great numbers.[1]

And Allāh (ﷻ) bestowed great numbers upon the children of Israel. He said,

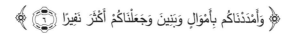

﴿ وَأَمْدَدْنَاكُم بِأَمْوَالٍ وَبَنِينَ وَجَعَلْنَاكُمْ أَكْثَرَ نَفِيرًا ﴿٦﴾ ﴾

---

[1] Narrated by 'Abū Dāwūd, 2050; Al-Nasā'i, 3227; classed as authentic by Shaykh al-Albānī.

And We reinforced you with wealth and sons and made you more numerous in manpower.[1]

Shuaib mentioned the numbers of his people. He said,

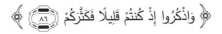

And remember when you were but few, and He multiplied you.[2]

The attempt to decrease the offspring of the Muslims is an attempt from the enemies of Islām; whether it be from the hypocrites who pretend to be Muslims or from the disbelievers who openly display their animosity toward the Muslims. Sometimes it may be necessary to reduce the number of births so the mother is not harmed. In this case, we say there is no problem with this and we take the lesser of two harms. The companions use to engage in coitus interruptus during the lifetime of the Prophet (ﷺ), and he did not forbid them from doing this.[3] The Messenger of Allāh (ﷺ) was asked about coitus interruptus and he said,

---

[1] Sūrah al-'Isrā' 17:6.

[2] Sūrah al-'A'rāf 7:86.

[3] Jābir ibn 'Abdullāh (ﷺ) said, "We used to engage in coitus interruptus at the time of the Messenger of Allāh (ﷺ). News of that reached the Messenger of Allāh (ﷺ) and he did not forbid us to do that. Narrated by *Al-Bukhārī*, 250 and *Muslim*, 160.

That is the subtle way of burying infants alive.[1]

This shows that it is permissible although it contains that which is disliked.

Shaykh 'Uthaymīn (🙏) went on to say, "I'd like to take an opportunity to discuss a phenomenon which was mentioned to us. It is that many of the obstetricians in the hospitals—male and female—are eager for childbirths to take place by way of a surgical procedure known as a cesarean section. I fear this is a plot against the Muslims. This is because the more births take place in this manner, the more the skin of the abdomen is weakened. Pregnancy becomes more dangerous for the woman, and she becomes unable to get pregnant. Some of the people who work in private hospitals have told me that many times a woman will go to the hospital and her specialist informs her that she has no alternative to cesarean birth. Then she goes to a private hospital and has a natural birth. He mentioned that there were about 80 cases like this in the span of one month. This means this affair is serious and attention must be drawn to this, attention must be drawn to this. It must be noted that pain during childbirth is inevitable, and exhaustion is inevitable.

Allah (🙏) said,

$$\text{﴿ ﴿ ١٥ ﴾ حَمَلَتْهُ أُمُّهُ كُرْهاً وَوَضَعَتْهُ كُرْهاً ﴾}$$

---

[1] *Ṣaḥīḥ Muslim* 1442.

His mother carried him with hardship and gave birth to him with hardship. [1]

It is not proper that as soon as the woman feels contractions she goes and removes the child (by cesarean) so she doesn't feel the pain anymore. Therefore, natural childbirth is better than cesarean. But if she experiences some unnatural hardship; then goes to the hospital for a cesarean birth while trying to avoid it to the best of her ability, this is permissible."[2]

Four: Medical Treatment Abroad

One of the salafi brothers in our *masjid* said he continued searching for treatment for his son, to remove a malignant tumor in his back that was causing him severe pain. He could not find the proper treatment until the "German Mission" agreed to take his son to Germany for prerequisite therapy under one condition. The condition was that no one could travel with him to Germany. He asked my advice. Thus, I warned him against this travel and explained to him the dangers facing his son in his religion and worldly affairs.

Five: Medical Experimentation

From the startling actions of the missionaries is what some of them mentioned in a book concerning Christianization. The medical missionaries utilize their missions to conduct medical experiments to test

---

[1] Sūrah al Ahqaf 46:15.
[2] Open sitting with Shaykh 'Uthaymīn (☼).

food and drugs which will be used in western societies. They test the medicines on Muslims before they test them on rabbits and mice. Then they send the reports to the food banks and pharmaceutical companies to approve the medicine and dispose of the people.

Translator's Addendum

———

EVIL MEDICAL EXPERIMENTS CONDUCTED ON HUMANS

One: The Tuskegee experiments in Alabama, from 1932 to 1972, called the Tuskegee Study of Untreated Syphilis in the Negro Male

Three hundred ninety-nine syphilitic patients, most of them poor, black, illiterate sharecroppers, were not told they had syphilis. They were denied treatment or given fake placebo treatments.

Two: The Aversion Project in South Africa from 1971 to 1989

Homosexual men were taken to Ward 22 and given chemical castrations and electric shock treatment to cure them of homosexuality. As many as 900 homosexuals were surgically turned into "women" against their will, then cast out into the world. The head of this project, Dr. Aubrey Levin, was tried and convicted of sexually assaulting male patients and subsequently, his license was suspended.

Three: Guatemala syphilis experiment conducted in Guatemala from 1946 to 1948

The experiments were led by United States Public Health Service physician John Charles Cutler. United States-led human experiments turned syphilitic prostitutes loose on Guatemalan prison inmates, mental patients, and soldiers, none of whom consented to be subjects of an experiment. In 2010, Secretary of State Hillary Clinton formally apologized to Guatemala for this dark chapter in American history.

Four: Agent Orange experiments from 1965 to 1966

Dr. Albert Kligman, funded by Dow Chemical, Johnson & Johnson, and the U.S. Army, conducted what was deemed "dermatological research" on approximately 75 prisoners. What was actually being studied was the effects of Agent Orange on humans.

Five: Irradiation of black cancer patients

Between 1960 and 1971, the Department of Defense funded non-consensual whole-body radiation experiments on poor, black cancer patients, who were not told what was being done to them. Patients were exposed, in the period of one hour, to the equivalent of about 20,000 x-rays worth of radiation.

Six: The Monster Study

The Monster Study was a stuttering experiment performed on 22 orphan children in Davenport, Iowa in 1939. It was conducted by Wendell Johnson at the University of Iowa. Half of the children received positive speech therapy, praising the fluency of their speech. The other half received negative speech therapy, belittling the children for speech imperfections. Many of the normal-speaking orphan children who received negative therapy in the experiment suffered negative psychological effects and some retained speech problems for the rest of their lives.

Seven: Project 4.1

Project 4.1 was the designation for a medical study conducted by the United States of the residents of the Marshall Islands who were exposed to radioactive fallout from the March 1, 1954 Castle Bravo nuclear test at Bikini Atoll. Instead of informing the residents of the island of their exposure, and treating the victims while they studied them, the U.S. elected instead just to watch quietly and see what happened. (Sources: Larry Schwartz and Encyclopedia)

End of Translator's Addendum

Chapter Four

FINANCIAL AND PHYSICAL EFFORTS OF CHRISTIAN MISSIONARIES

One: Budget of Christian missionaries

The Christianization budget around the globe for the year 1990 C.E. was around 164 billion U.S. dollars, in that year alone! This was reported in the Saudi publication *Dawah* by one of the African tourism officials. In 1992, that figure jumped to 181 billion U.S. dollars. While speaking on Christianization, a lecturer noted this was an increase of 17 billion dollars in just two years. The disparity in numbers is due to the number of missionaries, missionary institutes, meetings, conferences, and other means of "Christianizing."

Two: Missionary Organizations

The number of missionary organizations in the world has been listed at 24,580. The number of general service organizations has been listed at 20,700. Also, the number of organizations that send evangelization specialists to relief areas has been listed at 3,880.

Three: Missionary Institutes

The number of missionary institutes exceeds 98,720, while the number of full-time missionaries who work outside of the Christian community is more than 273,770.

Four: Books

The number of books authored for the purpose of Christianization exceeds 22,100, written in various languages and dialects. The number of pamphlets and regular periodicals is 2,270, distributed to millions in different languages.

Five: Radio Stations

The number of evangelistic radio stations is 1,900. They broadcast to more than 100 countries in 100 languages. In a treatise entitled *Missionary Radio Directed Toward Arab Muslims*, it states that there are more than 35 radio stations around the world, including *Vatican Radio* in more than 47 languages. Thirty-four of them are basic languages, while 13 of them are only used on special occasions. They increased the number of Arabic broadcasts to 1,500 per week, nearly 80,000 hours per year.

Six: Bibles

Sixty-four million copies of the Bible were printed in 1984. A shipload of Bibles entered the port of Algeria, but the government refused them entry.

MUSLIM CONVERTS TO CHRISTIANITY

With a call this massive, its colossal efforts and enormous amounts of money, there is no doubt there will be victims. I saw several benefits in mentioning the number of victims. From these benefits is to alert the Muslims to the danger of this call. And with Allāh lies all success.

❖ The call to Christianization converted 500,000 Muslims in Kazakhstan to Christianity in less than 20 years.

❖ In 2004, more than 2,000 Moroccans converted to Christianity.

❖ One hundred twenty Yemeni Muslims, from one province, converted to Christianity. This is the same number of Muslims who converted by way of the Jibla Hospital, bringing the total to 240 Yemeni Muslims.

❖ Some evangelists in Egypt say more than 3,000 Muslims have converted to Christianity, while others say the number is 10,000. This number was stated in the field report about the Christianization of Egypt.

❖ The impact of Christianization upon Indonesia has decreased the Muslim population from 95% to 86%. This is proof that the number of Christians is increasing there.

We ask Allāh (ﷻ) for safety and security.

THE ROLE OF INTERNATIONAL ORGANIZATIONS

Events have proven that despite the different agendas of various international organizations, they all proceed according to guidance from the West in dealing with others. Some authorities authored a released report in 1995 concerning the serious activity of international missionary organizations in Africa. Their slogan was "Leave the religion of Islām and we will save you from hunger, poverty, fear, and disease." The reported missionaries formed armies across Africa carrying food in their left hand and the cross in their right hand. According to Dr. Muḥammad As-Salumi in his book *Innocent Victims*, Columbia International University of America has a special role in preparing graduates and employing them after graduation to evangelize the Muslim world, whether through global relief organizations or another disguise. The University provides cover and stealth means to facilitate evangelizing Muslims. This was mentioned in an article in *Mother Jones Magazine* in 2002. It has been reported that weapons were placed in wheat bags sent by international organizations to Southern Sudan to assist the rebels lead by John Garang.

Translator's Addendum

Excerpts from article: "The Stealth Crusade" by Barry Yeoman, May/June 2002 Issue

Inside one southern university, Christian missionaries are trained to go undercover in the Muslim world and win converts for Jesus. Their stated goal: to wipe out Islām.

These students, all evangelical Christians, have arrived two weeks early for an intensive course on how to win converts in Islāmic countries. They're learning from the master. Rick Love is the international director of Frontiers, the largest Christian group in the world, that focuses exclusively on proselytizing to Muslims. With 800 missionaries in 50 countries, Frontiers' reach extends from the South Pacific to North Africa, and every major Islāmic region in between.

Love's lesson for today is how to mask one's identity while secretly working to convert Muslims.

Their zeal is helping to fuel the biggest evangelical foray into the Muslim world since missionary pioneer Samuel Zwemer declared Islām a "dying religion" in 1916, and predicted that "when the crescent wanes, the Cross will prove dominant."

"We see Islām as the final frontier," says David Cashin, a professor of Intercultural Studies at CIU who used to don Muslim clothing and pursue converts in the tea shops of Kaliakoir, Bangladesh. Like many of his fellow evangelicals, Cashin regards the Islāmic world as a hinterland that must be penetrated before the Messiah can return.

Missionaries themselves acknowledge that their work endangers the lives of converts, and critics charge that it disrupts the delivery of humanitarian aid and fuels the resentment of Westerners. But to those at the heart of the movement, including Rick Love's students, any damage done by their work is outweighed by the importance of their mission—to wipe out Islām.

CIU is one of three schools in the United States with a degree program specifically devoted to converting Muslims.

"My goal is not to convert a Muslim," says Al-Dobra, a 45-year-old with a gravelly voice and military haircut who befriends Muslim businessmen in Nairobi, Kenya, and then tries to convince them of Islām's fallacies. "My goal is to plant a tiny seed that will fester and gnaw and grow so that eventually they will begin to question their religion. My prayer is that they will become restless sleepers and troubled by what they hear."

Missionaries today are more likely to take on Muslim names, dress in veils and other local clothing, prostrate themselves during prayer, and even fast during Ramadan. "We must become Muslims to reach Muslims," says Cashin, the CIU professor.

In Jordan, the missionaries had "Jesus mosques." They called themselves "Muslims of the Messiah."

End of Translator's Addendum

A DEPICTION OF THE DANGER OF CHRISTIANIZATION

In order to give a clear picture of the danger of Christianization upon the Muslim community and the individual, we give an example of what occurred in Senegal as a result of Christianization and how it impacted the Muslims. The Christian population in Senegal does not exceed 1%; but despite this, the Christians today rule over the Muslims. From the effects of Christianization there are:

❖ Christianization is in full swing in Senegal, with hundreds of missionary organizations operating there. There, they find no difficulty in fulfilling their mission. The rich Muslim kids go to their schools to receive their education. And there is a demand for hospitals bearing the Red Cross emblem, at a time when no hospitals bear the Red Cross logo.

❖ Friday, *Jumu'ah*, is a workday in Senegal. The official days off there are Saturday and Sunday. The Muslims get two hours on Friday to perform *Jumu'ah* prayer if they stay late on Tuesday, Wednesday, and Thursday to make up for these two hours on Friday.

❖ The Christian holidays are public holidays, not Eid al-Fitr and Eid al-Adha. Christianization in Senegal strives to separate the Muslim from his religion so it will not play a role in his life and he will think it better to be Christian.

❖ Arabic was the first official language of Senegal before it was conquered. After that, it was illegal to spread it for a long time.

❖ Christianization has, likewise, spread among the pagan tribes. They prefer them to remain idol worshipers than for them to embrace Islām, but Islām is the religion most of the pagans embrace.

❖ There has been much talk about turning Dakar, the capital of Senegal, into the headquarters of Zionism in West Africa.

Chapter Five

CHRISTIANIZATION IN YEMEN

The conversation surrounding Christianization in Yemen is important to us, but I shall summarize for you some points.

❖ The first evangelist work from the missionaries took place in the city of Aden in Southern Yemen during the 1950s, according to the Christian calendar. As for Northern Yemen, their first efforts were in 1390 Hijri, which coincides with 1970 C.E. These efforts were started by the guerrilla organization known as Red Sea Mission Team,[1] founded by missionary Lionel Gurney in 1951 C.E. They called themselves "tentmakers."[2] These are Christians who go to

---

[1] Currently known as "Reach Across," their mission statement states, "We share the Gospel with Muslims. We serve them in practical ways. We disciple them to follow Jesus."

[2] Tentmaking refers to a method of international Christian evangelism in which missionaries support themselves by working full-time in the marketplace with their skills and education instead of receiving financial support from a Church. They

Muslim countries and work in various professions, such as doctors, teachers, and nurses. Their slogan is "Islām must hear us." Their objective is to circulate Bibles amongst the Muslims. Their headquarters is located in England, and they receive the support of churches, Christian organizations, and individuals to help this team with a number of development projects in numerous Muslim countries and across Africa, such as Mali, Djibouti, Pakistan, Yemen, and Tanzania. And they receive the approval of the host country.

❖ In 1992 C.E., two Yemenis in the province of Jibla—close to the city of Ibb and south of the Yemeni capital of Sanaa—ripped pages out of the Noble Qur'ān and tossed them into the bathrooms of Al-Ashrafiyyah Masjid. This crime shook the Yemeni community. After questioning, they admitted in court that they had apostated from Islām and converted to Christianity at the hand of a Christian. This transpired after they began reading and studying the Bible with him. One of the three pointed out that the main focus of the movement was to Christianize one of the doctors working in Jibla Baptist Hospital, as well as some of the foreign nationals. He said they were promised money in exchange for Christianizing Muslims.

❖ A Somolian Muslim living in the refugee camps in Aden converted to Christianity because of the civil war in his country. He converted at the hand of a foreign priest working in the city. He told him to change his name in the presence of the Yemeni immigration

---

claim that Paul supported himself by making tents while living and preaching in Corinth.

officials. He was arrested; but before he could be taken to trial, he received humanitarian asylum through the priest. And he converted another Somolian recently.

❖ Christianization activity in Yemen occurs through churches—although rare—and by way of hospitals, maternity wards, centers for disability services, language centers, academic scholarships, and tourism. They prey on Yemenis and mostly Somali refugees. There are more than 150,000 Somalis living in Yemen, of whom more than 50,000 are registered with the United Nations High Commissioner for Refugees (UNHCR), giving the evangelists ample space and fertile ground to operate. It is noteworthy to mention that this group has made several gains after 1990 C.E. due to the following reasons.

- They took advantage of the unification of Yemen which occurred in 1990.[1] This allowed national and voluntary organizations to work on a large scale with little supervision.

- The deteriorating economy in Yemen following the second Gulf War,[2] in which hundreds of thousands of Yemeni workers in the Gulf States were returned to Yemen, caused an increase in the poverty rate.

---

[1] Yemeni unification took place on May 22, 1990 when the area of the People's Democratic Republic of Yemen (also known as South Yemen) was united with the Yemen Arab Republic (also known as North Yemen), forming the Republic of Yemen (known simply as Yemen).

[2] Since Yemen held a seat on the United Nations Security Council, its reluctance to authorize forces to oust Iraq from Kuwait was particularly noteworthy. Saudi Arabia, in retribution, compelled hundreds of thousands of Yemeni workers to leave the kingdom.

- Hundreds of thousands of Somalis were displaced from their country following the civil war in Yemen, and waves of displacement continue albeit at lower rates.

- Other factors, include poor health care, widespread diseases, and inadequate education, have also strengthened the efforts of the UNHCR.

The Christianization of Yemen moves on two fronts.

First: Proselytizing to some Yemenis and implicitly telling them to leave Islām. They present to them the package that Christianity is the savior for mankind and all their woes. They exploit the poverty of the people, and some of the authorities do favors for the missionaries by filling out special-purpose forms for them.

Second: They try to corrupt the youth and shake their faith in Islām through various enticements such as taking them on field trips, and to concerts, film screenings, and trips to learn English abroad. An example of this is that eight years ago, a woman named Susan Alexander, originally of Egyptian origin, visited Aden. She is a member of the Finnish Evangelical Mission. During her visit, she focused on young men and women under the guise of attending to their needs. She had them conduct a survey for the University of Helsinki of Finland, which contained many suspicious questions, some of which were directed toward the young girls. The young girls were asked questions such as:

∴ What do you wear outside of the home, a scarf, jacket, *ḥijab*, bandanna, face veil, or no face veil?

❖ Would you like to work outside the home? What time do you awake and what time do you go to bed?

This woman visited some of the middle schools and showed the kids some pornographic pictures and asked them to comment on them. She then asked them if they had ever seen pornographic films or practiced masturbation!!!

THE MOST PROMINENT CHURCHES AND ORGANIZATIONS IN YEMEN

There are many Christianization efforts present in Yemen. We will focus on the most important of them.

1. The Catholic Church in Tawahi[1] is the most important church in terms of location. It has been opened since the 1950s, during the British presence in Aden. It is, perhaps, the most important church built in the Arabian Peninsula. It was reopened with a medical center in 1995 by the U.S. embassy in Sanaa. This annex exploits the people by providing surgeries, glasses, and other items at cheap prices. I say, "This church is half a kilometer or less from our *masjid*, and the people flock there for treatment. I still remember to this day, a brother came to me in the year 1417 Hijri (1997 C.E.) with two books. One entitled *The Bible: The Word of God* and *World*

---

[1] St. Anthony Church in the province of Tawahi, Aden.

Aflame.[1] He said, "It was distributed in the church by credible people."

2. American Baptist International Ministries. They are active in the Jibla Hospital, which has a strong connection to the church. Their activity extends to the province of Taiz, under the guise of concern for the poor, orphanages, and women's prisons. Some statistics reported that the American Baptist International Ministries at Jibla Hospital converted 120 Muslims to Christianity. Some of the churches distribute the Bible and Christian magazines, as well as audio and videotapes. For example, a cruise ship visited Aden in 1999 C.E., distributing the Bible and a magazine inviting the Muslims to embrace Christianity.

3. Doctors Without Borders[2] are medical missionaries who invite people to embrace Christianity. They tempt them with money and take advantage of the people's needs and their poverty.

4. Missionaries of Charity[3] are active in Taiz and Al-Ḥudaydah, especially in treating those afflicted with leprosy and mental illness. They

---

[1] William Franklin "Billy" Graham, Jr., (1965).

[2] Doctors Without Borders or Médecins Sans Frontières (MSF) is a non-profitable international medical humanitarian organization created in 1971 by doctors and journalists in France. MSF gives emergency aid to people in areas where there is no health care available, as well as those affected by wars, epidemics, famine, natural disasters, and man-made disasters. It provides this help to all people, regardless of their race, religion, or political beliefs. (Encyclopedia).

[3] The Missionaries of Charity is a Roman Catholic religious congregation established in 1950 by Mother Teresa.

have a strong connection with the Indian[1] nun Mother Teresa. This mission is connected to an extension of a well-known hospital in the capital of Yemen, Sanaa. At this mission, there are 10 nuns and they oversee the psychiatric care unit in the province of Al-Ḥudaydah, as well as the infirmaries in Sanaa and Taiz.

5. Academic Canadian Institute teaches English as a cover for their activities. They are known for their discount prices in relation to the other foreign language institutes. Their program incorporates field trips, concerts, and mixed-gender studies. The students continue with their Canadian teachers, even after they return to their countries. They engage the students in discussions that include raising doubts about Islām. The efforts to expose these institutions and alert the public to their hidden dangers and agendas can be considered minimal at best. This is because most of the efforts are from individuals such as scholars and students of knowledge. There are efforts to educate the African and Asian students living in Yemen. A commission was established for this purpose, called the Islām Presentation Committee. It is based in Sanaa and has a center in the city of Ibb.

CHRISTIANIZATION WEBSITES ON THE INTERNET

The following information was narrated from the website marebpress.net, which mentioned some Christianization websites such as

---

[1] When asked about her personal history, Mother Teresa said, "By blood, I am Albanian, by citizenship, an Indian. (*Just Spirituality: How Faith Practices Fuel Social Action,* InterVarsity Press).

"Yemen for Christ." Their objective is to spread Christianity to the people. The managing editor of this website is a Yemeni national in his 20s who posts under the pseudonym "Son of Sanaa." He uses a pseudonym fearing he will be declared an apostate he if does not. He wrote, "I married an Arab Christian woman and I work in a western country. I embraced Christianity while I was in Yemen, and I was also baptized in Yemen." He mentioned that, at his baptism, he bore witness to the father, the son, and the holy spirit. Son of Sanaa also said the number of Christian Yemenis reached 2,500, and there are 700 of them outside of Yemen. He said, "There are families there (Yemen) who are Yemeni Christians, and their children were born into Christianity. We constantly communicate with each other, either by phone or online." He went on to say the Christians practice their religion each week in congregation in one of their homes, either a Yemeni national or a foreigner. Likewise, they strive hard to Christianize the young men and women. He said, "It is difficult to change the Yemeni laws because most of the country is Muslim, and we don't have any political objective." He also mentioned that he and two of his friends built the website. He clarified that the purpose of the website was to explain the Christian religion to the people of Yemen and save them from spiritual death. He said, "We hope to see the house of the Lord on the ground here in Yemen."

We seek refuge in Allāh (﷾) from disbelief and the means that lead to it.

MISSIONARY ORGANIZATIONS

❖ Millennium Relief Organization. This is an American Christianization organization. Its first and last objective is to Christianize the
people. They use humanitarian work as a cover for their suspicious
goals. This organization operates globally. Its lone branch in Yemen
is in Sanaa, in front of the Mali Institute. They have a group of
foreign evangelists with them. At the head of them is Dennis Cox,
known as 'Abū Dāwūd. He has lived in Yemen for over 25 years,[1]
such that he is considered the mastermind of Christianization in
Yemen. He has the greatest animosity and hatred toward Islām and
the Muslims. He was the architect who devised a campaign to insult
the Prophet (ﷺ) and the Noble Qur'ān. This program began three
years ago with the introduction of several books, CDs, and tapes that
are offensive to Islām and the noble Prophet (ﷺ).

❖ Global Cooperation Partnership. This is a Christianization organi-
zation that operates in Yemen. It is run by the American evangelist
Allen Pascovich and his German wife, Sofia. Its headquarters is in
Sanaa.

❖ The International Social Service (ISS). This is the missionary organization that follows the Baptist church that oversaw Jibla Hospital.
They are active in several provinces in Yemen and have an institute
to teach English on the Yemeni island of Socotra. It is run by the
American evangelist Drew Watson. This information has all been
posted on the website factway.net.

---

[1] Dennis Cox first worked in Yemen in 1983, with Sheibani Associated Companies.

OTHER CHRISTIANIZATION CAMPAIGNS

The missionary activities have become a phenomenon, especially with foreigners choosing to live in the heritage buildings in the city. The foreigners who live there distribute the Bible to the residents, in addition to Christian publications that incite the practice of Christianity and encourage the Muslims to leave Islām. The only youth who respond to this are the needy or rebellious. One man mentioned, "There are questions as to how some of the youth get rich quick, having homes, cars and taking trips. These are the same youth who spend much of their time with foreigners." He went on to say, "Some of the foreigners tried to convince me to embrace Christianity. I refused, and we had many discussions about Islām.

A translator who works for an official institution confirmed that three years ago, during his university studies, they had attempted to evangelize him by luring him with money and studying abroad. One Yemeni said, "The attempts to Christianize him were not only by foreign Christian missionaries, but the missionaries were also accompanied by Yemeni youth.

YEMENI CHRISTIANS

Before we conclude this topic, we point out that there is a Christian minority in Yemen that holds Yemeni nationality. They are a small number of families with Indian origins and have resided in Aden for several decades. They came from their British occupied country with the intention to live in southern Yemen. There are some Yemeni nationals who converted to Christianity after having been Muslims. They remained upon apostasy until they died as Christians. They were buried along with the British in Maala Cemetery which includes the remains of many English Christians. The Church of Christ, in the town of Tawahi, supervises this cemetery.

One time an old man knocked on the door after midnight. He told me that he came to ask about his daughter's husband who was working in the Kingdom of Saudi Arabia; and then, went from the kingdom to a neighboring Gulf country, where he converted to Christianity. We seek refuge with Allāh (﷽) from disbelief and its causes. This proves there are those who enter Christianity due to external causes and factors, not just from the missionaries in Yemen.

As for the places of Christian worship, the Anglican Catholic Church (the Church of Christ) is located in Aden, within Tawahi City. It is an old church that dates to the 1950s during the British presence in Aden. This church is affiliated with the Church of Cyprus Synod of the Autocephalous Church of Cyprus.[1] This church follows the ecumenical council in Larnaca, Cyprus; but since its reopening in 1995, it is still being managed temporarily by the Anglican administration in Dubai, United Arab Emirates. The church has a medical center attached to it that provides health services. It was bombed in April 2002.

---

[1] Translator's note: The Holy Synod of the Autocephalous Church of Cyprus is the highest church authority in Cyprus. Its task is to examine and provide solutions on all issues concerning the Church of Cyprus.

Until recently, there was a Baptist church in Crater City, within Aden. However, it was closed, and its building was turned into a government facility. The northern provinces do not contain churches; but foreign Christians regularly perform Sunday prayers in private homes, especially in Sanaa (the capital city of Yemen). In general, the Yemeni Christians are prohibited from carrying out Christianization operations; and for this reason, some sources indicate that the messages of Christian clerics are regularly monitored.

HOW DO WE FACE THE DANGER OF CHRISTIANIZA-TION?

We would like to first explain the importance of facing the danger of Christianization. It is a communal responsibility. Thus, everyone in a position of responsibility—the rulers, subjects (male and female), callers, and others—is responsible. But there are important things that must be considered to confront this Christianization. The most important matters are as follows.

1. We must circulate the correct, sound religious creed and clarify the clear misguidance and deviance the Christians are upon, along with their major plots against the Muslims.

2. We must revive the creed of loyalty and disavowal.

3. Go out to give *dawah*—invite people to the path of Allāh (ﷻ)—in the villages and countryside, as these are the cracks by which they enter. These are the places by which evil enters upon us because these are the focal points of the Christians.

4. It is obligatory upon us to recognize the gravity of this affair and the great responsibility before Allāh (ﷻ). Indeed, Allāh (ﷻ) will question all of us—those in authority, those under their authority, the rulers, and the community. He will question all of us about this religion and the souls that leave monotheism and go to disbelief and total darkness. We must take a serious stand against this danger. We must use all of our efforts to prevent this creeping tide that has come against the Muslim lands. The leaders—may Allāh guide them to what He is pleased with—have much responsibility.

❖ The rulers must scrutinize these Christian organizations. Those whom they feel are calling to Christianity must be struck with an iron fist so they are not tempted to invite anyone to Christianity in the future. We ask Allāh (ﷻ) to protect His religion and elevate His Word.

❖ The rulers must understand that the reason many Muslims turn toward these Christian organizations is due to an urgent need they have, especially in terms of medicine and health care. So they must close this door by providing hospitals and the necessary health care so the Muslims do not have to go to the Christians.

❖ They must block all Christianization websites to the best of their ability. These websites are far more dangerous than pornographic websites. Some of these websites are from outside of Yemen. Others are inside of Yemen, such as the website *Yemen for Christ*, and a church forum titled *The Church of the Children of Yemen*. Protecting the religion of the Muslims is from the greatest intent of the Islāmic Sharī'ah.

CONCLUSION

CONCLUSION

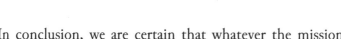

In conclusion, we are certain that whatever the missionaries do, they will fail. We ask Allāh (ﷻ) to guide them to Islām; otherwise, their efforts will be a disappointment and their plots will be pushed in their throats. The failure of their efforts is affirmed by the following.

∴ It was stated by Walter Stanley Mooneyham (1926-1991), during a 1978 missionary conference held in America, "The publications of missionaries working among Muslims are full of phrases such as, "lack of response," "difficult area," "slow growth," or "rough terrain." He also said, "For months we have been involved in a Christianization campaign in the city of Chiang Mai. The campaign was part of a celebration for the 150th anniversary of the start of Christianization there. This city is considered the Christian center in northern Thailand, and the Bible reached it 110 years ago. Nevertheless, the Christians in this city are still a small, depressed minority.

∴ Even when they are victorious in evangelizing some people, Allāh (ﷻ) causes crowds of others to abandon Christianity and enter the religion of pure monotheism and true faith. Thus, all praises belong to Allāh (ﷻ). There is a major difference between the person who enters Islām with strong conviction—being influenced by the greatness of Islām and the biography of the Messenger of Allāh (ﷺ)—and the person who enters the misguidance of Christianity because he is poor and in need; thus, he turns away from his religion and his Lord. It is such that the Christians see it as necessary to keep their followers away from Islām due to the large number of them who have embraced it.

❖ Everyone who falls into their traps, then upon him is a portion of their sin until the Day of Judgment. Allāh (ﷺ) spoke the truth when He said:

$$ ﴿ إِنَّ الَّذِينَ كَفَرُوا يُنفِقُونَ أَمْوَالَهُمْ لِيَصُدُّوا عَن سَبِيلِ اللَّهِ ۚ فَسَيُنفِقُونَهَا ثُمَّ تَكُونُ عَلَيْهِمْ حَسْرَةً ثُمَّ يُغْلَبُونَ ﴿٣٦﴾ ﴾ $$

Verily, those who disbelieve spend their wealth to hinder (men) from the Path of Allāh, and so will they continue to spend it; but in the end, it will become an anguish for them.[1]

May Allāh (ﷺ) elevate the rank and send salām and blessings upon our Prophet Muḥammad, his family, and his companions.

---

[1] Sūrah al-'Anfāl 8:36.

CHRISTIANIZATION IN THE PHILIPPINES

Shaykh 'Abdul Azīz ibn Baz (☀)

Question: A brother from the Philippines asked, "From the means to Christianize Muslims in the Philippines is to offer them financial support. Under the guise of spiritual support, they send priests to the Imām and his congregation. They deliver a lecture about mixing Islām and Christianity in place of the Friday sermon. That happens weekly. How do we deal with this? May Allāh (☀) reward you with good.

Answer: It is obligatory upon those responsible for the affairs of the Muslims, the scholars and others, to intervene between them and their plots. They must put forth strong efforts to help the Muslims so they will have no need for support from their enemies. They must warn against the machinations of the enemies. They must encourage the Muslims to be patient and diligent in staying away from their enemies and avoid mixing with them and listening to their advice. For indeed, they are inviting them to the Hellfire, while the people of Islām are inviting them to Paradise.

It is upon the believer to be patient and seek the reward from Allāh (☀). They must be patient with the hardships they may endure due to their weakness and needs until their situation improves. It is a duty upon their Muslim brothers to comfort them, treat them with kindness, and assist them with all available means, even if they only have a little. Because if many people give a little it becomes a lot. This person gives what he can, and that person gives what he can. Consequently, the good that is given will accumulate. Those in need will benefit from the Muslims and they will not be exposed to the evil of their enemies and their plots and schemes, those who lie waiting to ambush them. This will free the Muslims from spending their money, money that will lead them to the Hellfire. We ask Allāh (ﷻ) for safety and security.

It is important that the leaders of the Islāmic minorities, and also the elders, write to those who are upon good and explain to them the need of their poor brothers. They should seek help from the leaders of Islāmic centers and Islāmic associations so everyone can cooperate upon good. They cannot be heedless of this. It is a duty upon everyone to cooperate upon righteousness and piety. They should assist them in finding good income and earnings that will help them upon the obedience of Allāh. They should help them find good jobs in their country that will benefit them so they will not need to receive help from their enemies. The Messenger of Allāh (ﷺ) said in an authentic *hadīth*,

احْرِصْ عَلَى مَا يَنْفَعُكَ وَاسْتَعِنْ بِاللهِ وَلاَ تَعْجِزْ

Be diligent upon that which benefits you, and seek the help of Allāh, and do not become weak.[1]

This *hadīth* has been collected in Saḥīḥ Muslim. It is upon the believer to strive in seeking provision, and he must seek permissible provision so he will have no need of seeking help from the enemies of Allāh (ﷻ).[2]

---

[1] *Saḥīḥ Muslim* 2664.
[2] *Religious Verdicts and Lessons*, Fatwa 2963.

THE PERMANENT COMMITTEE FOR RESEARCH AND VERDICTS' WARNING AGAINST CHRISTIANIZATION

All praises belong to Allāh, the Lord of all that exists. May Allāh exalt the rank and send peace upon the man sent as a mercy for the creation, the seal of the prophets and messengers, our Prophet and Messenger Muḥammad, and upon his family, his companions, and those that follow him upon goodness until the Day of Judgment. As to what follows:

It is not hidden from anyone whom Allāh has enlightened his heart with insight, the extreme animosity that the disbelievers—from the Jews, Christians, and others—have against the Muslims. They unite their forces against the Muslims to turn them away from their true religion, the religion of Islām that Allāh (﷾) sent to all of creation, by way of the seal of the prophets, Muḥammad (ﷺ). The disbelievers have various plots to deceive the Muslims and colonize their minds. Their efforts and harms are intensified during the present time. One of their misleading plots was to send a brochure called *English Language Institute in South Africa*. These leaflets were sent through the mail to individuals and institutions. They were sent to the Arabian Peninsula, the origin and stronghold of Islām. Included in this brochure were correspondence study programs and a subscription card for free books. These books were the Old Testament, New Testament, and Book of Psalms. On the back of these brochures were excerpts from all these books. It is from the glad tidings for the Muslims in this worldly life to denounce this organized onslaught and warn against it with all means. From these refutations is the writing from the Standing Committee for Academic Research and Issuing Fatwas. Thus, we say, and with Allāh (﷾) lies all success, since the sun of Islām first shined upon the earth, while its enemies were upon different creeds and plotted day and night against it. They schemed and took every opportunity to move the Muslims from the light into the darkness, undermine Islāmic countries, and weaken Islām's authority over their souls. This illustrates the statement of Allāh (ﷻ) when He said,

﴾ مَّا يَوَدُّ الَّذِينَ كَفَرُوا مِنْ أَهْلِ الْكِتَابِ وَلَا الْمُشْرِكِينَ أَن يُنَزَّلَ عَلَيْكُم مِّنْ خَيْرٍ مِّن رَّبِّكُمْ ﴿١٠٥﴾ ﴾

Neither those who disbelieve from the People of the Scripture nor the polytheists wish that any good should be sent down to you from your Lord.[1]

And the statement of Allāh (ﷻ),

﴾ وَدَّ كَثِيرٌ مِّنْ أَهْلِ الْكِتَابِ لَوْ يَرُدُّونَكُم مِّن بَعْدِ إِيمَانِكُمْ كُفَّارًا حَسَدًا مِّنْ عِندِ أَنفُسِهِم مِّن بَعْدِ مَا تَبَيَّنَ لَهُمُ الْحَقُّ ﴿١٠٩﴾ ﴾

Many of the People of the Scripture wish they could turn you back to disbelief after you have believed, out of envy from themselves [even] after the truth has become clear to them.[2]

---

[1] Sūrah al-Baqarah 2:105.
[2] Sūrah al-Baqarah 2:109.

And Allāh (﷾) said,

﴿ يَا أَيُّهَا الَّذِينَ آمَنُوا إِن تُطِيعُوا فَرِيقًا مِّنَ الَّذِينَ أُوتُوا الْكِتَابَ يَرُدُّوكُم

بَعْدَ إِيمَانِكُمْ كَافِرِينَ ﴿ ۞ ١٠٠ ۞ ﴾

O you who believe, if you obey a group of those who were given the Scripture, they would (indeed) render you disbelievers after you have believed![1]

From the most prominent enemies of this religion are the spiteful Christians, those who were and are still doing their best to resist the Islāmic tide in every corner of the world. Rather, they even attack Islām and the Muslims in their own lands, especially when the Muslim world is in a state of weakness, as is the case today. It is well-known that the intent of this attack is to shake the faith of the Muslims, causing them to doubt their religion This is in preparation to remove them from Islām while tempting them to convert to Christianity through what is mistakenly called evangelism. In reality, it is a call to paganism in the distorted religion of Christianity. Allāh (﷾) did not send down an authority for the religion they are upon today, and Jesus (ﷺ) has no association to them whatsoever. The Christians have spent large sums of money and exerted great effort to achieve their dreams of Christianizing the world in general, and Muslims in particular. But their situation is as Allāh (﷾) described it.

---

[1] Sūrah 'Āli 'Imrān 3:100.

﴿ إِنَّ الَّذِينَ كَفَرُوا يُنفِقُونَ أَمْوَالَهُمْ لِيَصُدُّوا عَن سَبِيلِ اللَّهِ ۚ فَسَيُنفِقُونَهَا ثُمَّ

تَكُونُ عَلَيْهِمْ حَسْرَةً ثُمَّ يُغْلَبُونَ ﴿٣٦﴾ ﴾

Verily, those who disbelieve spend their wealth to hinder (men) from the Path of Allāh, and so will they continue to spend it; but in the end it will become an anguish for them.[1]

To achieve their objective, they held several regional and global conferences, starting a century ago and continuing until the present day. Missionaries and workers flock from every part of the world to exchange ideas and suggestions on the most effective means. They collected the best results and designed plans and programs. Their plans included sending missionaries to Islāmic countries to call to Christianity by distributing publications, books, and pamphlets that teach Christianity. They also sent translations of the Bible and other publications to attack and distort Islām. Then they started Christianization using indirect methods. The following are some of their most dangerous methods.

Medical treatment: They provided medical care to the people. This method was effective due to the people's need for medical care and the proliferation of epidemics and deadly diseases in Islāmic countries, especially during the time when Muslim doctors were scarce. In fact, some countries do not have any Muslim doctors.

---

[1] Sūrah al-'Anfāl 8:36.

Education: Another means of Christianization was through education. This was either by establishing schools and universities that were clearly based upon Christianity or by opening schools which on the surface were purely educational centers with no religious affiliation, while in reality, it was a Christian school. Muslims placed their children in these centers due to their desire to learn a foreign language or some other desire. The Christians took advantage of this by giving the Muslim children gifts. Thus, they captured their hearts while they were young and impressionable.

Media: This is done through radio broadcasts directed to the Islāmic world. Also, there is the visual flood that has come by way of satellite television in recent years, not to mention newspapers, magazines, and bulletin boards.

They call to Christianity by displaying its illusionary virtues, mercy, and compassion for the entire world.

They present doubts to the Muslims concerning their religious creed and religious practices.

They spread pornography to arouse the desires. The purpose of this is to reach those who are heedless and destroy their morals, modesty, and chastity. Thus, transforming them into people who worship their desires and seekers of cheap pleasures. Once this occurs, it becomes easy to invite them to anything, even apostasy and disbelieving in Allāh (ﷻ). And with Allāh (ﷻ) refuge is sought. This occurs after faith has faded within their hearts and the protective barrier in their souls has collapsed.

There are other means that they utilize to Christianize the Islāmic world. These means are evident to those given insight. However, we shall suffice with this summary because the intent is to warn against their plans, not to detail all of their plans. Because the affair is as Allāh (ﷻ) has mentioned.

They were planning and Allāh too was planning, and Allāh is the Best of the planners.[1]

And Allāh (ﷻ) said,

﴿ يُرِيدُونَ أَن يُطْفِئُوا نُورَ اللَّهِ بِأَفْوَاهِهِمْ وَيَأْبَى اللَّهُ إِلَّا أَن يُتِمَّ نُورَهُ وَلَوْ كَرِهَ الْكَافِرُونَ ﴿٣٢﴾ ﴾

They want to extinguish the Light of Allāh with their mouths, but Allāh refuses except to perfect His light, although the disbelievers hate it.[2]

These are the plots of the missionaries and their plans to deceive the Muslims. So, what is the duty of the Muslims in response to this? How do we respond to these fierce attacks against Islām and the Muslims?

---

[1] Sūrah al-'Anfāl 8:30.
[2] Sūrah at-Tawbah 9:32.

There is no doubt that the responsibility is great and shared—among all the Muslims, individuals and groups, and governments—to stand up to this poisonous encroachment that targets every member of the Muslim 'ummah, young and old, male and female. Allāh, alone, is Sufficient for us, and He (ﷻ) is the Best Disposer of affairs for us.

We can mention, in general, the steps that must be taken while keeping in mind every situation will have its particular circumstances.

1. Establish the Islāmic creed within the hearts of the Muslims through educational curricula and programs, while placing emphasis on entrenching it in the hearts of the youth, especially those in the private and public school system.

2. Circulate the proper religious awareness among the entire 'ummah regardless of social status. Entice the people to have jealousy for the religion and its sanctities.

3. Focus on the outlets by which missionary materials enter—films, publications, and magazines—and prevent them from entering. Also, impose a penalty as a deterrent on those who violate this.

4. Make the people aware of the plots of Christianization and the missionaries, so they can avoid falling into their traps.

5. Pay special attention to every aspect of the Muslim's life and necessities. This especially applies to health and education, because these are the outlets the Christians use to enter the hearts and minds of the people.

6. Each and every Muslim in every place on the earth must adhere to his religion and his belief, regardless of the situation or his circumstances. He must establish the rights of Islām within himself and those under his care to the best of his ability. His household must be fortified to resist every onslaught that attacks their beliefs and morals.

7. Each individual and family must beware of traveling to the lands of the disbelievers unless there is an urgent medical need or necessary knowledge that cannot be found in the Muslim lands. If they travel to these lands, they must possess the ability to repel the doubts and religious tribulations directed toward the Muslims.

8. The Muslims must be active in cooperating such that the rich fulfill the rights of the poor and take care of their needs. This way the polluted hands of the Christians do not reach out to them and take advantage of their poverty.

In conclusion, we ask Allāh, the Generous, by His Beautiful Names and Lofty Attributes, to unite the hearts of the Muslims, bring about reconciliation among them, and guide them to the path of safety. We ask Him (💫) to protect them from the plots of the enemy and their evil, and to distance them from their tribulations, those that are apparent and those that are hidden. Indeed, He is the Most Merciful.[1]

---

[1] *Religious Verdicts and Important Matters*, 15.

IMPORTANT FIGURES IN THE CHRISTIANIZATION CRUSADES

Translator's Addendum

∴ Ramon Llull (1232-1315), from Spain, is the first Christian to start missionary work after the failed crusades. He learned the Arabic language and began traveling through Sham to debate with Muslim scholars. He traveled throughout Europe to meet with popes, kings, and princes, trying to establish special colleges to prepare future missionaries.[1]

∴ William Carey (1761-1834) was known as the father of modern missionaries. He founded the Particular Baptist Society for the Propagation of the Gospel Amongst the Heathen, subsequently known as the "Baptist Missionary Society." He spent 41 years in India as a missionary. Carey Baptist Church, in Reading, England, is named after him.

∴ Henry Martyn (1781-1812) was an Anglican priest and missionary to the peoples of India and Persia. He translated the New Testament into Urdu, Persian.

∴ David Livingstone (1813-1873) was a Scottish physician and Christian missionary with the London Missionary Society in central Africa. Livingstone is known as "Africa's greatest missionary," although he is recorded as having converted only one African.

---

[1] *Paul Richard Blum: Philosophy of Religion in the Renaissance.*

Livingstone College, a private, historically black Christian college in Salisbury, North Carolina, is named after him.

❖ Samuel Marinus Zwemer (1867-1952), nicknamed "The Apostle to Islām," was an American missionary born in Vriesland, Michigan. He was head of the Arab Missionary Mission in Bahrain and President of Christianization Societies in the Middle East. He is the founder of American Mission Hospital in Bahrain. He established the quarterly magazine *The Moslem World* in 1911. The Zwemer Institute was established in his name in America to research the Christianization of Muslims.

❖ Kenneth Cragg (1913-2012) was an Anglican bishop. He was chaplain of All Saints Church in Beirut, as well as Professor of Arabic and Islāmic studies at Hartford Seminary and warden of St. Augustine's College, Canterbury. He wrote numerous books aimed at Christianizing Muslims, such as *Sandals at the Mosque, Jesus and the Muslim,* and *The Call of the Minaret.*

❖ Louis Massignon (1883-1962) was a Catholic. He sponsored evangelization and Christianization in Egypt and was a member of the Academy of the Arabic Language in Cairo. He was also the advisor to the French Colonial Ministry on North African affairs.

❖ Daniel Bliss (1823-1916), from Vermont, was a Christian missionary from the United States and the founder of the American University of Beirut, formerly known as the Syrian Protestant College. This University was established to prepare missionaries.

❖ Stephen B.L. Penrose, Jr. was the president of The American University of Beirut from 1948 until 1954. He said, "Evidence has led to education being the most valuable tool used by American missionaries in their quest to Christianize Syria and Lebanon."

∴ Donald Hoke (1919-2006) was a Protestant ordained minister from Chicago. He was the Director of the 1974 International Congress on World Evangelization in Lausanne, Switzerland. He worked as a missionary in Pakistan for twenty years. In 1978, he became director of the Zwemer Institute.

CHRISTIANIZATION CONFERENCES

Christians have held numerous Christianization conferences throughout history and they continue to do so.

∴ The Cairo Conference in 1906. Zwemer called for this conference with the aim of bringing together Protestant missionaries to discuss spreading the gospel among Muslims. The conference was attended by 62 men and women, with Zwemer as the chairman.

∴ The 1910 International Missionary Conference, in Edinburgh, Scotland, was attended by representatives of 159 missionary societies in the world.

∴ The 1911 Evangelization Conference in Lucknow, India was attended by Samuel Zwemer. After the conference ended, leaflets were distributed to the members. One side of the leaflet read "Lucknow memento 1911." The other side read "O God, whoever in the Islāmic world prostrates five times a day, with reverence, I look to the Islāmic people with compassion inspired by salvation through Jesus Christ."

SECRET SOCIETIES: FREEMASONS, ILLUMINATI AND MISSIONARIES

- Missionary Conferences in Jerusalem in 1924

- International Missionary Conference in Mount Olives, Jerusalem in 1928

- Baltimore, Maryland conference in 1942, which was attended by David Ben-Gurion (1886-1973), the primary national founder of the State of Israel and the first Prime Minister of Israel

- Amsterdam Conference 1948, Netherlands

- Protestant Churches Conference in Lausanne, Switzerland in 1974

- The 1975 Jakarta Conference in Indonesia, in which 3,000 Christian missionaries participated

- The North American Conference on Muslim Evangelization, held in Colorado Springs in October 1978, was the most dangerous. It was attended by 150 participants, representing the most active missionary elements in the world. It was a closed forum format. Comprehensive research papers were presented on how to convey the gospel to Muslims and inform them about the incarnation of Christ and his love of the Muslim heart. They discussed means to evangelize Muslims, analyze Muslim resistance, and how to utilize food and health as two elements in Christianizing Muslims. They also discussed plans to revitalize the role of local churches in Christianizing the Islāmic world. The conference ended with the development of a strategy that was kept secret because of its seriousness. The budget for this plan was one billion dollars. This amount was collected and deposited in one of the major American banks.

❖ The Sixth Conference of the World Council of Churches was held in July 1980, in California. The conference urged the necessity of increasing missionaries among Muslims in the Middle East, especially in the Arab Gulf states.

❖ The International Conference on Christianization, held in Sweden in October 1981, under the supervision of the Lutheran Federal Council. The results of the Lausanne and Colorado conferences were discussed, and a comprehensive study on overseas Christianization was developed to focus on third world countries.

Other conferences include the Istanbul Conference, Helwan Conference in Egypt, Lebanon Missionary Conference, The Missionary Conference of Lebanon, and The Constantine Missionary Conference in Algeria. After WWII, the Church decided to hold a missionary conference every six or seven years in rotating countries.

MOST FAMOUS CHRISTIAN MISSIONARY ASSOCIATIONS AND INSTITUTES

❖ London Missionary Society, founded in 1795

❖ The Zwemer Center for Muslim Studies in California. The decision to open this center was made after the Colorado Conference.

❖ The International Center for Research and Evangelism in California

❖ The American University of Beirut (formerly the Syrian Protestant College), established in 1865

❖ The American University in Cairo was established to compete with Al-Azhar. It was founded in 1919 by American Mission in Egypt, a Protestant mission sponsored by the United Presbyterian Church of North America.

❖ The Church Mission Society (CMS), founded in 1799, is a British mission society working with the Anglican Communion and Protestant Christians around the world.

❖ The American Missionary Association (AMA), a Protestant-based abolitionist group founded on September 3, 1846, in Albany, New York

❖ The Berlin Missionary Society (BMS) or Society for the Advance-ment of Evangelistic Missions Amongst the Heathen, founded in 1824.

❖ YMCA, the Young Men's Christian Association, was established in 1855. Their stated mission is to introduce the kingdom of Christ to young men.

❖ World Student Christian Federation, formed in 1895